HAL LEONARD
GUITAR METHOD
Supplement to Any Guitar Method

ROCKABIL

BY FRED SOKOLOW

Speed • Pitch • Balance • Loop

To access audio visit:
www.halleonard.com/mylibrary

Enter Code
5399-8716-6738-0423

with editorial assistance by Ronnie Schiff

ISBN 978-1-4234-9318-1

7777 W. BLUEMOUND RD. P.O. BOX 13819 MILWAUKEE, WI 53213

Visit Hal Leonard Online at
www.halleonard.com

CONTENTS

	PAGE	TRACK
INTRODUCTION	4	
About the Audio	4	
PRELIMINARIES	5	
The Role of Guitar in Rockabilly & Which Guitars to Use	5	
Amps & Delay Pedals	6	
Fingerpicks & Flatpicks	6	
Great Players to Listen To	7	
ACCOMPANIMENT	8	
Moderate Shuffle-Beat Strum	8	
"Boppin' the Blues"	8	1
Fast Shuffle-Beat Strum	9	2
"Milk Cow Blues"	9	2
Straight-Eighths Strum	10	3
"Train Kept A-Rollin'"	10	3
"American Music"	11	4
First-Position Boogie Bass Lines	11	5
"Boppin' the Blues"	12	5–7
"Honey Don't"	14	8
"Dance to the Bop"	15	9
Deadstring Boogie Bass Lines	16	
"Rock This Town"	16	10
"Get Rhythm"	17	11
Double-Note Boogie Bass Lines	18	12
"No Particular Place to Go"	18	12
"Dance to the Bop"	19	13
The 12-Bar Blues Form	19	
I–IV–V Chord Families	20	
Moveable Single-Note Boogie Bass Lines	21	14
"Boppin' the Blues"	22	15
"Honey Don't"	22	16
Moveable Double-Note Boogie Bass Lines	23	
"No Particular Place to Go"	23	17
"Dance to the Bop"	24	18
Fingerpicking Backup	24	19
"Good Rockin' Tonight"	25	19
"Susie-Q"	26	20
"Train Kept A-Rollin'"	27	21
"Milk Cow Blues"	28	22
"Boppin' the Blues"	30	23
Chop Chords	30	24
"Rock Around the Clock"	31	24
"Dance to the Bop"	31	25
Chord-Based Fills	32	
"Race with the Devil"	32	26
"Rock This Town"	33	27

	PAGE	TRACK
SOLOING	34	
First-Position E Minor Pentatonic Scale	34	
"I'm Lookin' for Someone to Love"	35	28
"Be-Bop-A-Lula"	36	29
The Moveable Blues Box	36	
"Be-Bop-A-Lula"	37	30–32
"Race with the Devil"	40	33
Chuck Berry-Style Double-Note Licks	40	34
"No Particular Place to Go"	41	34–35
"Dance to the Bop"	43	36
"American Music"	44	37
Chord-Based Soloing	44	
"Not Fade Away"	44	38
"Honey Don't"	45	39
"Boppin' the Blues"	46	40
Fingerpicking Solos	46	
"Susie-Q"	47	41
"Train Kept A-Rollin'"	48	42
"I'm Lookin' for Someone to Love"	48	43
"Good Rockin' Tonight"	49	44
"Milk Cow Blues"	50	45
"Be-Bop-A-Lula"	51	46
Swing-Style Single-Note Soloing	51	
"Race with the Devil"	52	47
"Rock Around the Clock"	53	48
"Rock This Town"	54	49
Octave Soloing	55	
"Train Kept A-Rollin'"	55	50
Psychobilly	56	
"Psychobilly Freakout"	56	51
Endings & Closing Chords: 6ths, 7ths, and 6/9 Chords	58	
"Boppin' the Blues"	58	52
"Honey Don't"	58	53
"Dance to the Bop"	58	54
"Rock Around the Clock"	59	55
"Be-Bop-A-Lula"	59	56
"Rock this Town"	59	57
"Race with the Devil"	59	58
WHERE TO GO FROM HERE	60	
ABOUT THE AUTHOR	61	
GUITAR NOTATION LEGEND	62	

INTRODUCTION

Welcome to the *Hal Leonard Rockabilly Guitar Method*! This book teaches the techniques, licks, chords, scales, and strums you need to play rockabilly guitar. It shows you how to play rhythm (backup) and lead for all kinds of rockabilly grooves. Instead of learning exercises, you learn the classic rockabilly songs and solos that made the genre come together in the first place. The recording that accompanies the book will help you catch the rhythms and nuances of the rockabilly style.

In case you're not clear on what *rockabilly* music is or how it started…

In the early 1950s, a new kind of music was evolving in the honky-tonks and roadhouses of the South. Young white bands were blending honky-tonk country music, boogie woogie, and R&B with a little bluegrass, western swing, and southern gospel mixed in. The result was a driving, frenetic music usually featuring an acoustic rhythm guitarist (who was often the lead singer), an upright bassist, an electric guitarist (who played loud, crazy solos), and a drummer who pushed the backbeat as hard as he could. It was a raw, stripped-down-to-basics sound with no frills and a killer dance beat.

In 1954, when Sun Records began releasing singles by Elvis Presley and his trio, the genre found its charismatic, iconic figurehead. The new sound spread like wildfire all over the South and beyond. At first, many called it "rockabilly," but Alan Freed and the other disc jockeys who promoted the new phenomenon knew it was really "race music" played by white kids. Many of the songs were covers of R&B or blues hits, and most of them had a boogie beat with a 12-bar blues form.

The guitarists of the era—Carl Perkins, Chuck Berry, Scotty Moore, James Burton, Buddy Holly, Eddie Cochran, Paul Burlison, Cliff Gallup—invented and defined rock 'n' roll guitar playing. Rockabilly guitar was, and still is, a melting pot of American guitar styles. It combines the fingerpicking acoustic styles of bluesmen like Lightnin' Hopkins, the electric, single-note blues solos of T-Bone Walker, the country-style fingerpicking of Merle Travis, and the electric solos of Charlie Christian and Bob Wills' western swing guitarists. This book shows you how these styles meld into rockabilly guitar.

In the 1980s, the Stray Cats spearheaded a rockabilly revival in the U.S., and many dance clubs featured rockabilly nights, when live bands played retro-style rock for dancers dressed in 1950s' styles. In Europe and Japan, rockabilly had never disappeared—a rockabilly cult has always existed there. The 1980s' craze subsided, but in big urban centers there are still rockabilly bands and clubs that feature them. Rockabilly revivals will come and go, but there will always be an audience for this music, and bands will keep playing the old tunes and making up new ones in the rockabilly style. I hope this book helps you be a part of that scene!

Good Luck!

ABOUT THE AUDIO 🔊

The accompanying audio contains demonstrations of many examples in this book. The corresponding track number for each song or example is listed below the audio icon. All notated guitar parts are panned to the right side of the stereo mix, so you can isolate them for close study or pan them out to play along with the band.

Guitars: Fred Sokolow
Bass, Drums, and Sound Engineering: Michael Monagan

Recorded at Sossity Sound

PRELIMINARIES

THE ROLE OF GUITAR IN ROCKABILLY & WHICH GUITARS TO USE

Electric guitar was always important in R&B bands, but it often took a backseat to the piano and horns. In rockabilly, *guitar has always been the driving force*. The rhythm guitar established a song's rhythmic feel; it was the foundation on which everything else was built. It was usually acoustic in the 1950s' bands, but subsequent rockabilly rhythm guitarists went electric, and their modern counterparts often play an *acoustic-electric* (an acoustic guitar with a built-in pickup). Most acoustic rhythm guitarists favor the steel-string dreadnought guitars (Elvis Presley played a Martin Dreadnought).

In most rockabilly bands, the electric guitar is the only soloing instrument. It can be any electric guitar, but actual vintage or retro-style guitars are popular—especially ones played by the early rockabilly greats. Brian Setzer favors the Gretsch 6120 hollowbody because that's what Eddie Cochran played. Others like the Gretsch Duo Jet that Cliff Gallup popularized or the Fender Telecaster that was James Burton's trademark. You'll see rockabilly lead guitarists playing 1940s and '50s hollow- and semi-hollowbody Gibson guitars (like Scotty Moore's Gibson ES-295) with single-coil P-90 pickups and a single cutaway (or not) because that's what many original rockabilly cats played!

Martin D-28

Gretsch 6120
hollowbody

Gretsch Duo Jet

Fender Telecaster

Gibson ES-295

AMPS & DELAY PEDALS

Electric guitars need amplifiers, and rockabilly guitarists tend to prefer tube (like the Tweed Fender Bassman) over solid state amps, as the latter weren't invented when rockabilly was born. *Tube amps* have a warmer sound and more natural distortion. Early Fender tube amps are popular, but any vintage or modern tube amp will do. Many old amps are now recreated by contemporary manufacturers and they look and sound like the originals.

Fender Hot Rod-Deluxe

Fender Bassman

Scotty Moore, James Burton, and a few other pioneering rockabilly lead guitarists had a tape-loop device built into their amps. This created a delay effect that resembled the unusual style of echo Sam Phillips produced in Memphis' Sun Studio. Today's rockabilly guitarists often imitate this sound by using a *delay pedal*. These pedals, or "stomp boxes," create single or multiple repeats of the notes you play. Usually, they have several knobs that allow you to adjust the speed of the repeated signal (the length of the delay), its volume (relative to the note you play), and the number of repeats. For a rockabilly sound, you want a single repeat that comes a split second after the note you play (known as a "slapback" delay), and you want this repeated note to equal the original note in volume.

Boss Digital Delay
DD-6

FINGERPICKS & FLATPICKS

Since fingerpicking is an important part of rockabilly lead guitar, many players wear metal *fingerpicks* and a plastic *thumb pick*. The thumb picks come in various sizes, and the metal fingerpicks are bendable so they can fit any size fingers. They are worn as shown in the photo below, and they protrude about an 1/8 of an inch from your fingertips.

Fingerpicks and Thumb Pick

Wearing Picks

Many players, including Brian Setzer and James Burton, prefer playing with a *flatpick*. Instead of using their thumb for bass notes and index and/or middle fingers on the treble strings, the flatpick acts like the thumb, and the middle finger plays the treble strings—some call this *hybrid picking*. Burton wears a fingerpick on his middle finger in combination with the flatpick, while Setzer palms the flatpick in order to switch to "bare thumb and fingers" fingerpicking.

Holding Pick

GREAT PLAYERS TO LISTEN TO

Many rockabilly pioneers have already been mentioned: Carl Perkins, Scotty Moore (on most of the 1950s and early 1960s Elvis Presley recordings), Cliff Gallup (on Gene Vincent recordings), Eddie Cochran, Buddy Holly, Paul Burlison (with the Rock and Roll Trio), and James Burton (on Ricky Nelson's early hits, as well as Elvis Presley's and Emmy Lou Harris's 1970s recordings). Joe Maphis, who also played on some of Ricky Nelson's songs, was another pioneer of the style. So was Nashville's Grady Martin, who played on countless country classics of the 1950s, but was also lead guitarist on many early rockabilly recordings. Sun Records' compilations from the 1950s feature other lesser-known guitarists who are worth listening to as well.

Many consider Chuck Berry a rockabilly guitarist, and he was certainly a huge influence on all the rockabilly players. Link Wray, Duane Eddy, Luther Perkins (with Johnny Cash), and Roy Buchanan are also included in many lists of great rockabilly players. Also, listen to the guitarists of Dale Hawkins, Billy Lee Riley, and Wanda Jackson.

The Next Generation

Brian Setzer's recordings, with and without the Stray Cats, are full of brilliant guitar solos. Other rockabilly-influenced bands and guitarists include John Fogerty (with and without Creedence Clearwater Revival), Dave Alvin and the Blasters, Albert Lee (with Roseanne Cash and many other musical acts), Ray Flacke (with Ricky Skaggs and others), Danny Gatton, Vince Gordon (with the Holland band, the Jime), and Big Sandy and His Fly-Rite Boys.

Psychobilly is a hybrid of punk and rockabilly—it's nastier, noisier, simpler, and angrier than traditional rockabilly. Reverend Horton Heat is the most famous practitioner, along with Bamboula, the Raygun Cowboys, and Season of Nightmares. Some consider the Cramps and the Meteors pioneers of the genre.

Now let's get into the nuts and bolts of rockabilly guitar, starting with accompaniment!

ACCOMPANIMENT

Rockabilly rhythm guitarists usually strum full, first-position chords on an acoustic guitar. There are several possible rhythmic grooves.

MODERATE SHUFFLE-BEAT STRUM

This is the rhythmic feel of "Honey Don't," "Boppin' the Blues" (the way Carl Perkins' brother played it on acoustic rhythm guitar), "Blue Suede Shoes," and "Rock Around the Clock." You alternate down- and upstrokes, with eight strokes to a measure of 4/4 time. If you count, "1–&–2–&–3–&–4–&," the numbers are downstrokes, and the "&s" are upstrokes. There's an emphasis on beats 2 and 4 (both are downstrokes).

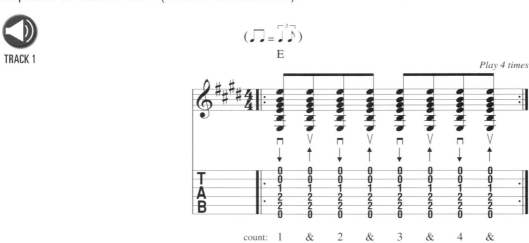

Here's the rhythm guitar part for the verse of "Boppin' the Blues."

BOPPIN' THE BLUES—RHYTHM GUITAR

Words and Music by Carl Lee Perkins and Howard Griffin

FAST SHUFFLE-BEAT STRUM

Some people call it "cut time." You hear this groove in Elvis's "Mystery Train" and "Milk Cow Blues," both from the Sun Sessions. In order to speed up the moderate shuffle beat, rhythm guitarists often leave out the first upstroke, creating this strumming pattern.

TRACK 2

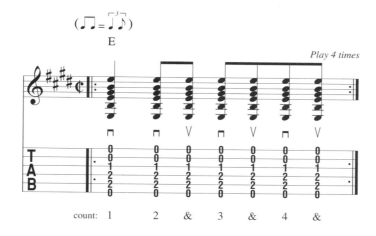

One time around "Milk Cow Blues" will give you a good sense of this rhythm groove.

MILK COW BLUES—RHYTHM GUITAR

TRACK 2
(0:08)

STRAIGHT-EIGHTHS STRUM

Most early rock hits had a shuffle beat, but the straight-eighths feel was also present in rock from the beginning, notably in songs like Little Richard's "Lucille," the Rock and Roll Trio's "Train Kept A-Rollin'," and Chuck Berry's "Johnny B. Goode" and "Nadine." Eventually, it became *the* rock beat.

One way for a rhythm guitarist to achieve this groove is to play eight downstrokes to a measure, with an emphasis (or *accent* <) on the third and seventh strokes (the second and fourth beats of the measure).

TRACK 3

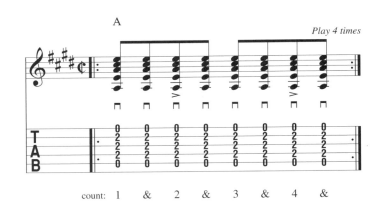

Here's what the rhythm guitar plays for the verse of "Train Kept A-Rollin'" (though it's barely audible in the original recording).

TRAIN KEPT A-ROLLIN'—RHYTHM GUITAR

TRACK 3
(0:10)

Words and Music by Tiny Bradshaw, Lois Mann and Howie Kay
Copyright © 1951 by Bienstock Publishing Company, Jerry Leiber Music, Mike Stoller Music, Fort Knox Music Inc. and Bug Music-Trio Music Company
Copyright Renewed
International Copyright Secured   All Rights Reserved
Used by Permission

TRACK 4

Sometimes, rhythm guitarists strum down- and upstrokes to get a fast, straight-eighths feel, as in the Blasters' "American Music." The Blasters were part of the Los Angeles punk scene in the 1980s, but their music (described in the song "American Music") was more rockabilly and R&B than punk.

AMERICAN MUSIC—RHYTHM GUITAR

TRACK 4
(0:30)

Written by Dave Alvin

FIRST-POSITION BOOGIE BASS LINES

Boogie woogie piano music is around a century old, and one of its key components is the unmistakable walking bass line that establishes the boogie rhythm. It's unclear whether that bass concept originated on guitar or piano, but it has long been played by guitarists in blues, R&B, and country music. It's usually played on tunes that are 12-bar or 8-bar blues forms.

Rockabilly lead guitarists often play boogie bass lines as accompaniment to vocals. They are played most often on songs in the keys of E and A, which are very popular rockabilly keys, but can be played in any key. There is an infinite variety of boogie bass lines, most of them based on the major scale notes "1, 3, 5, and 6." Here are two basic key-of-A patterns. The first is a one-measure pattern; the other is two measures long.

TRACK 5

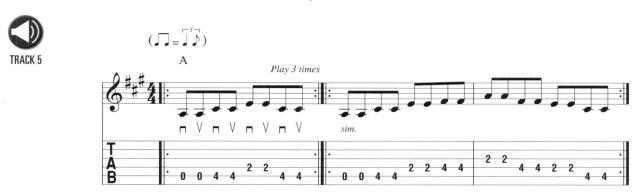

In the chorus of "Boppin' the Blues," Carl Perkins played a standard, one-measure boogie bass line. Notice how the pattern is moved "up a string" (to the fourth and third strings) for the D chord and "down a string" (to the sixth and fifth strings) for the E chord. Additionally, the last two measures sport an elongated, two-bar boogie phrase (incorporating the ♭7th, G♮, on beat 1 of the last measure).

BOPPIN' THE BLUES—BOOGIE BASS LINES

TRACK 5
(0:17)

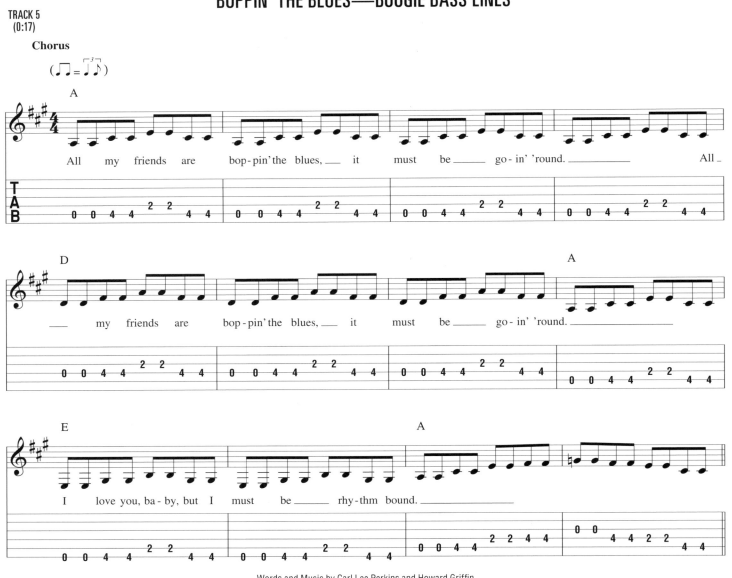

Here are some variations of the basic boogie bass line. Some are one-measure patterns, as in the previous examples, and some are two measures long. Some patterns include ♭3rds and/or ♭7ths, which are called *blue notes* (notes from the blues scale). Each pattern is played several times on the audio.

TRACK 6

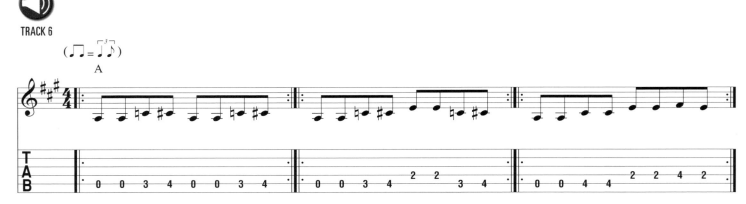

During the verses of "Boppin' the Blues," Perkins played a two-measure boogie bass line.

BOPPIN' THE BLUES—BOOGIE BASS LINES

Verse

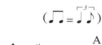

The doc - tor told me, "Carl, ___ you don't need no pills." Yeah, the

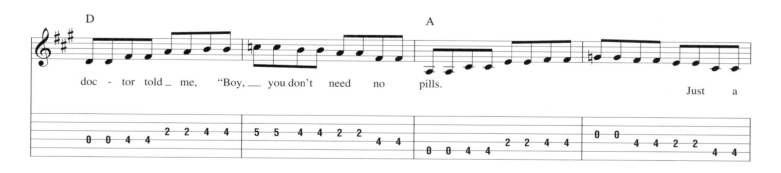

doc - tor told ___ me, "Boy, ___ you don't need no pills. Just a

hand - ful of nick - els in a _____ juke - box 'll cure your ills."

The chorus of Carl Perkins' "Honey Don't" features a two-measure boogie bass line in the key of E. Perkins strummed the B7 chord instead of continuing the boogie bass line to add some variety. The song was covered by the Beatles in the mid 1960s.

TRACK 8

HONEY DON'T—BOOGIE BASS LINES

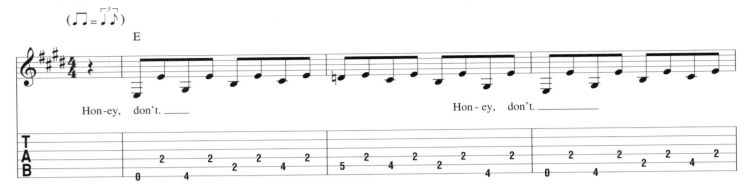

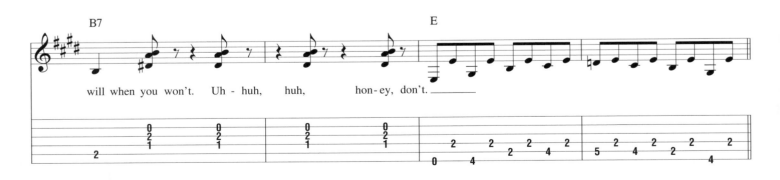

Words and Music by Carl Lee Perkins

In "Dance to the Bop," Gene Vincent's lead guitarist, Johnny Meeks, played two variants of the boogie bass line: one in the verse and another in the chorus.

DANCE TO THE BOP—BOOGIE BASS LINES

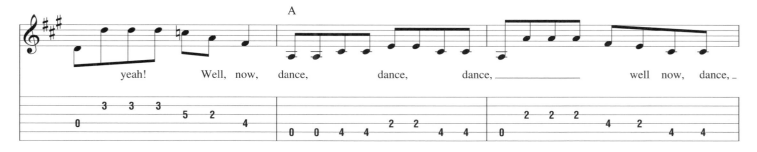

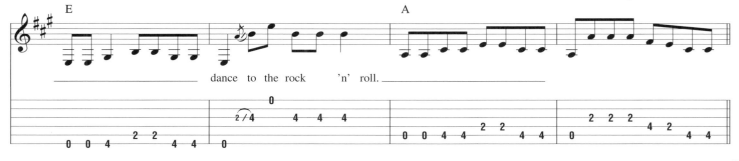

DEADSTRING BOOGIE BASS LINES

Sometimes, rockabilly lead guitarists create a percussive effect by playing boogie bass lines while muting the bass strings with the palm of their picking hand. This is often referred to as "deadstring" picking (or *palm muting*). Brian Setzer did it in the Stray Cats hit, "Rock This Town."

ROCK THIS TOWN—DEADSTRING BOOGIE BASS LINES

TRACK 10

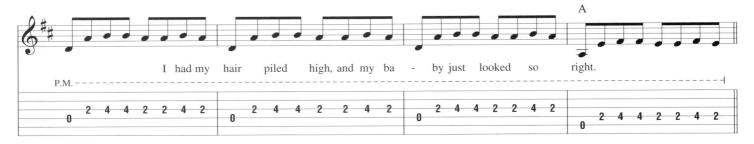

TRACK 10
(0:10)

Zeke Turner played deadstring boogie bass lines in the 1940s on Hank Williams' recordings. Luther Perkins (no relation to Carl), who played on the early Johnny Cash hits, was one of the first guitarists to popularize the technique in rockabilly music. He often backed up Cash songs with boogie bass lines like this one.

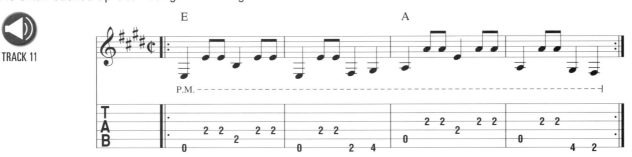

TRACK 11

In Cash's "Get Rhythm," Perkins played his typical country-style deadstring boogie bass lines during the verse and rockabilly-style lines during the chorus. The studio recording of the song is in the key of F, and video of Cash indicates that he and Luther Perkins tuned up a half step and played E, A, and B7 chords. Capo at fret 1 to match the recording.

GET RHYTHM—DEADSTRING BOOGIE BASS LINES

DOUBLE-NOTE BOOGIE BASS LINES

Here are some double-note boogie bass lines derived from the blues.

TRACK 12

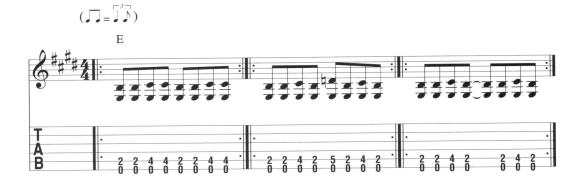

Chuck Berry popularized the blues guitar technique of playing double-note boogie bass lines. Typically, he used barre chords, but this style of backup comes from blues guitarists who played in first position, especially in the key of E. Here's how a chorus of Berry's "No Particular Place to Go" would be played in the first-position key of E.

NO PARTICULAR PLACE TO GO—DOUBLE-NOTE BOOGIE BASS LINES

TRACK 12
(0:21)

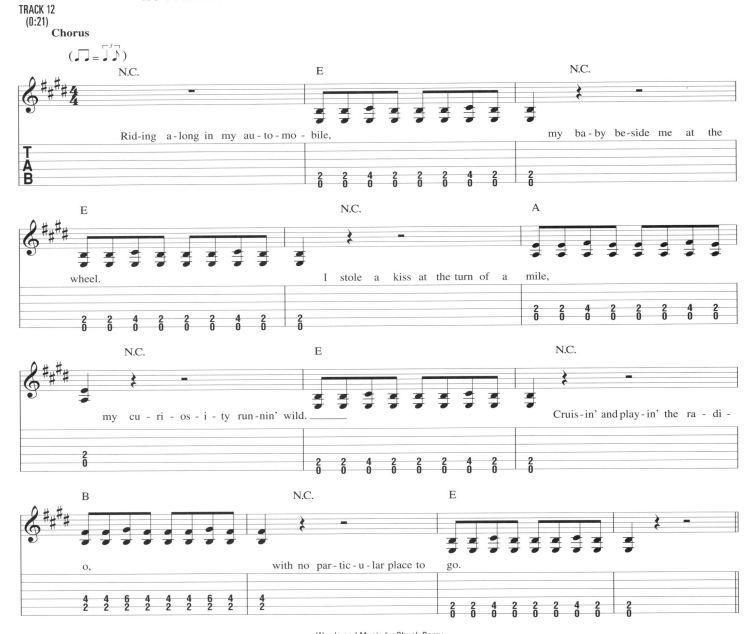

Words and Music by Chuck Berry
Copyright © 1964 (Renewed) by Arc Music Corp. (BMI)
Arc Music Corp. Administered by BMG Chrysalis for the world excluding Japan and Southeast Asia
All Rights Reserved   Used by Permission

The key of A also lends itself to double-note boogie bass lines. Here's how a rhythm guitarist might back up the chorus of "Dance to the Bop."

TRACK 13

DANCE TO THE BOP—DOUBLE-NOTE BOOGIE BASS LINES

By Floyd Edge
© 1957 (Renewed 1985) BEECHWOOD MUSIC CORP.
All Rights Reserved   International Copyright Secured   Used by Permission

THE 12-BAR BLUES FORM

Many early rockabilly songs use the *12-bar blues form*, or some variation of it, so it's essential to know how this popular chord progression works. While most pop, jazz, and country songs have chord patterns that are multiples of eight measures (16 measures, 32 measures, etc.), the 12-bar form, popularized first in blues songs, is popular in all the other genres as well. In its most stripped-down form, it consists of three four-measure phrases:

- Four measures of the I chord (A, in the key of A).

- Two measures of the IV chord (D, in the key of A), followed by two measures of I.

- Two measures of the V chord (E, in the key of A), followed by two measures of I.

The numbers (I, IV, and V) refer to the major scale of a song's key. If a song is in the key of A, A is the I chord, B, B7, or Bm (taken from the second note of the A major scale) is the II chord, and so on.

The lyrics of the second phrase are often a repeat of the first phrase. There are many variations of the above 12-bar format, such as this popular one:

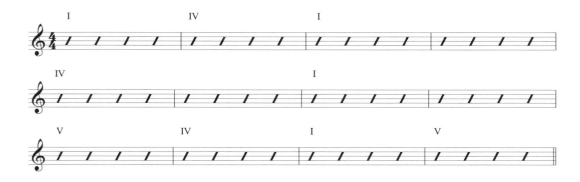

Some rockabilly and early rock songs that are 12-bar blues tunes (sometimes with slight variations) include "Blue Suede Shoes," "Whole Lotta Shakin' Goin' On," "Hound Dog," "Matchbox," "Lucille," "Peggy Sue," "Johnny B. Goode," "Long Tall Sally," "Good Golly Miss Molly," "School Days," "Back in the U.S.A.," "Tutti Frutti," "At the Hop," "Too Much," "Shake, Rattle and Roll," "Roll over Beethoven," and "Kansas City." Songs in this book that use the 12-bar blues form include "Rock Around the Clock," "Train Kept A-Rollin'," "Boppin' the Blues," "Milk Cow Blues," "I'm Lookin' for Someone to Love," "Be-Bop-A-Lula," "Race with the Devil," "Dance to the Bop," and "No Particular Place to Go."

I–IV–V CHORD FAMILIES

It has been mentioned already that the typical 12-bar blues consists of three chords: I, IV, and V. Countless rockabilly, rock, country, pop, and folk tunes also contain just these three chords. I, IV, and V are a *chord family*. They're the chords most likely to occur in any song. Here are the most common, first-position chord families:

I	IV	V
C	F	G
G	C	D
D	G	A
A	D	E
E	A	B

In blues tunes (and rockabilly tunes, which are mostly blues-based), *7th chords* are often played instead of major chords. The *9th chord*, which is just a fancier 7th chord, is often played as well. Here are two typical chord families, played with *moveable chords* (chords that have no open strings):

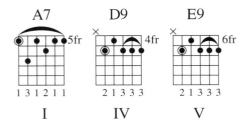

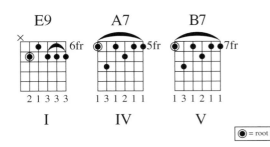

The relative positions of these chords are the same in any key:

- The V chord is always two frets above the IV chord.

- When the I chord has a sixth-string *root* (the note that gives the chord its name; an A note is the root of an A7 chord), the IV chord's root is at the same fret on the fifth string.

- When the I chord has a fifth-string root, the V chord's root is at the same fret on the sixth string.

Here are two more chord families that resemble the above two, moved up three frets:

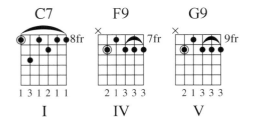

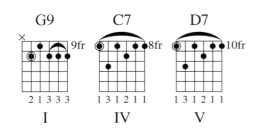

Once you're familiar with these two I–IV–V configurations, you can play in any key, up the neck, using moveable chords.

MOVEABLE SINGLE-NOTE BOOGIE BASS LINES

All the above boogie bass lines can be made moveable to be played in any key. Here's a basic, first-position boogie line transposed to other keys and played with moveable patterns. (If a lick or scale can be played on fretted strings only—no open strings—it's moveable and can be played in any key.)

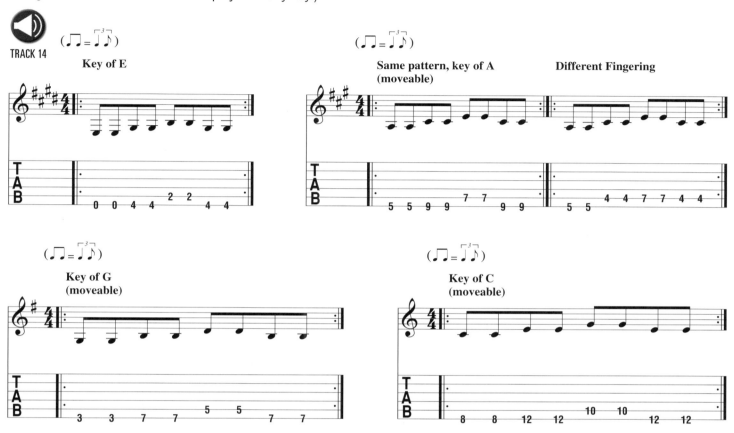

Two-measure patterns can also be played in moveable positions.

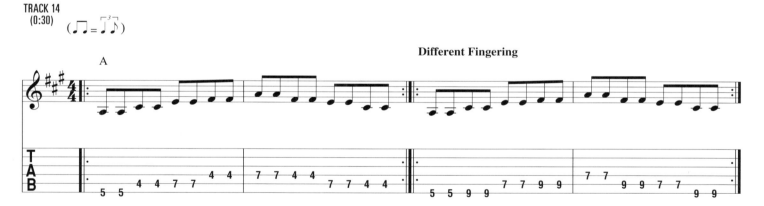

Any of the above patterns can be moved "up a string" (starting on the fifth string) to play the IV chord and "up a string and up two frets" to play the V chord. For example, here are two-measure boogie bass lines for A, D, and E chords (I, IV, and V in the key of A).

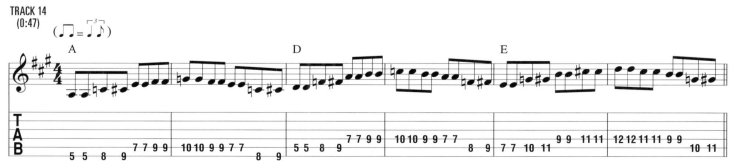

Here's how two of Carl Perkins' songs would sound in new keys, using moveable boogie bass lines.

BOPPIN' THE BLUES—MOVEABLE BOOGIE BASS LINES

TRACK 15

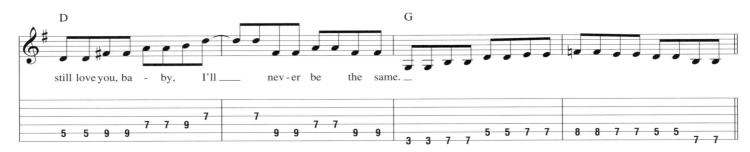

Words and Music by Carl Lee Perkins and Howard Griffin
© 1956 HI-LO MUSIC, INC.
© Renewed 1984 CARL PERKINS MUSIC, INC. (Administered by WREN MUSIC CO., A Division of MPL Music Publishing, Inc.) and HI-LO MUSIC, INC.
All Rights Reserved

HONEY DON'T—MOVEABLE BOOGIE BASS LINES

TRACK 16

Words and Music by Carl Lee Perkins
© 1955, 1956 HI-LO MUSIC, INC.
© Renewed 1983, 1984 CARL PERKINS MUSIC, INC. (Administered by WREN MUSIC CO., A Division of MPL Music Publishing, Inc.)
All Rights Reserved

MOVEABLE DOUBLE-NOTE BOOGIE BASS LINES

Using moveable, two-note chords that rock players call "power chords," the boogie bass lines notated a few tunes back (Double-Note Boogie Bass Lines, "No Particular Place to Go," and "Dance to the Bop") can be played in any key, all over the fretboard. Chuck Berry popularized this rhythm method, and rockers have been using it ever since. The power chords are simplified barre chords:

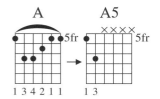
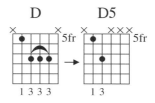

These chords are written with a "5" (e.g., A5 and E5) because they consist of a root and 5th, but no 3rd. Here are some of Chuck Berry's boogie bass lines on "No Particular Place to Go" in the key of G.

NO PARTICULAR PLACE TO GO—MOVEABLE DOUBLE-NOTE BOOGIE BASS LINES

TRACK 17

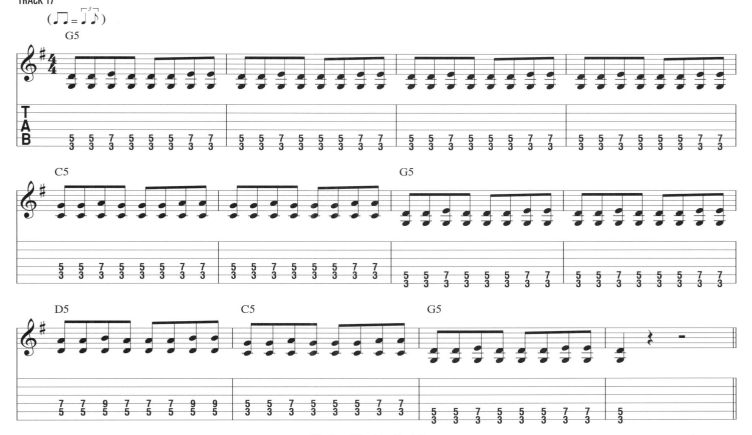

Words and Music by Chuck Berry
Copyright © 1964 (Renewed) by Arc Music Corp. (BMI)
Arc Music Corp. Administered by BMG Chrysalis for the world excluding Japan and Southeast Asia
All Rights Reserved   Used by Permission

The chorus of "Dance to the Bop" can be backed up with this moveable double-note boogie bass line.

DANCE TO THE BOP—MOVEABLE DOUBLE-NOTE BOOGIE BASS LINES

TRACK 18

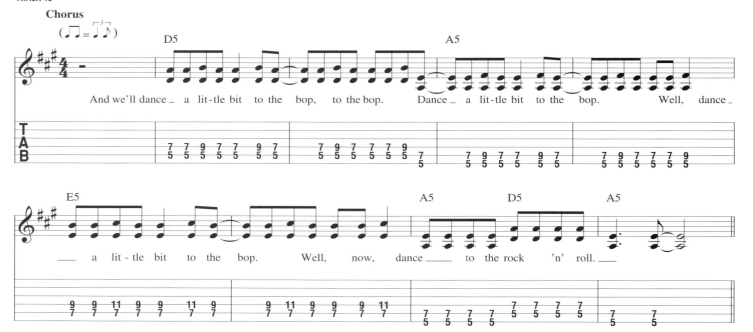

FINGERPICKING BACKUP

First-Position Alternating Bass

Fingerpicking electric lead guitar (with a delay effect) has always been one of the trademarks of rockabilly guitar. It started in 1954 when Sun Records producer, Sam Phillips, got two of his local musician pals, Scotty Moore and Bill Black (upright bassist), to bring the young, unknown singer Elvis Presley to his studio and "try him out" on some tunes. Phillips got excited by the trio's version of "That's All Right Mama," a 1940s R&B tune by guitarist/singer Arthur Crudup, and decided to make a record right away, even though there was no drummer present. The lack of percussion made Moore want to fill more holes than usual, so he put away his flatpick and fished the thumb pick and fingerpicks out of his pocket that he had been using at home to practice Merle Travis licks. Blues guitarists had used those fingerpicking licks, popularized by Travis, for decades, but they had a unique echo in Phillips' studio and fattened up the trio's sound more than single-note solos ever could.

Carl Perkins fingerpicked on "Blue Suede Shoes" and his other Sun recordings. When he was a sharecropper in Arkansas, a black neighbor taught him some fingerpicking guitar licks. Perkins became so adept at the style that he often fingerpicked while singing. Once the world had heard Elvis's and Perkins' records, most subsequent rockabilly guitarists added some fingerpicking to their solos and backup.

In the fingerpicking patterns that follow, the thumb alternates picking the bass strings, while the fingers pick treble strings. Play each pattern over and over until it sounds like the recording, and then play them in a sequence, over and over, as written. (Note: Many fingerpickers stabilize their picking hand by putting their ring and pinky fingers on the guitar, just below the strings.)

TRACK 19

Scotty Moore's backup in "Good Rockin' Tonight" makes use of these patterns, as well as a number of variations.

GOOD ROCKIN' TONIGHT—BACKUP

First-Position Monotone Bass

Fingerpicking with an alternating bass is associated with rockabilly music and the country stylings of Merle Travis and Chet Atkins, and "raggy blues" picking, à la Mississippi John Hurt, Blind Blake, Reverend Gary Davis, and a number of other African-American acoustic blues musicians. Ultimately, it comes from blues guitarists who first recorded in the 1930s. The other main strain of fingerpicking, which has a monotone bass, also comes from blues players as diverse as Robert Johnson, Lightnin' Hopkins, and Big Bill Broonzy.

In *monotone* bass picking, the thumb keeps playing the same root note, while fingers play the melody. In the original "Susie-Q," James Burton played a monotone bass riff throughout the tune—an E blues figure many have compared to the guitar riff that drives Howlin' Wolf's "Smokestack Lightning." Practice the lick over and over, playing all the notes with your index finger, except the low-E bass note. Once you can pick the melody easily, add the bass notes.

TRACK 20

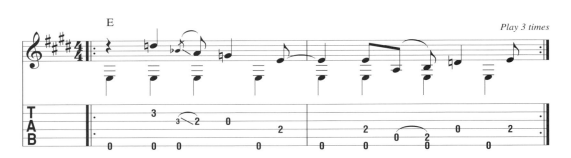

When first attempting this type of fingerpicking, most people find that playing melody notes throws the thumb off track. In monotone and alternating bass fingerpicking, the thumb has to become automatic, so you can concentrate on melody notes. Learning any one piece of music with this technique helps, even if you have to play one measure at a time, over and over, until it's comfortable and familiar. After you memorize a few tunes, it gets easier! Some people find it helpful to learn the melodic part first with their fingers, and then add in the thumb.

The original "Susie-Q" recording, released in 1958, was by Dale Hawkins with a teenage James Burton playing lead guitar. Creedence Clearwater Revival had a late-1960s hit with the song. Here's the backup part to a verse of "Susie-Q."

SUSIE-Q—MONOTONE BASS

TRACK 20
(0:17)

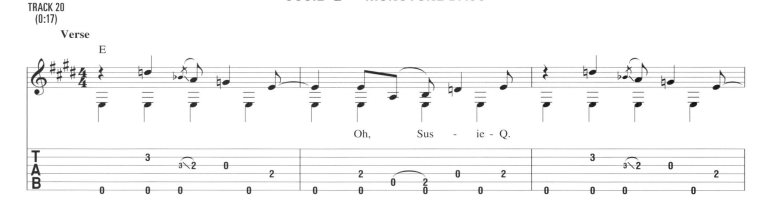

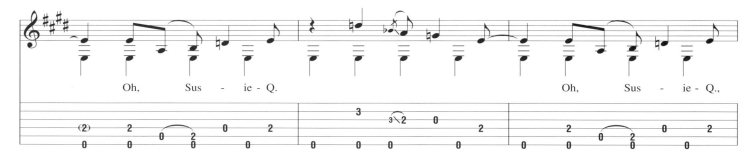

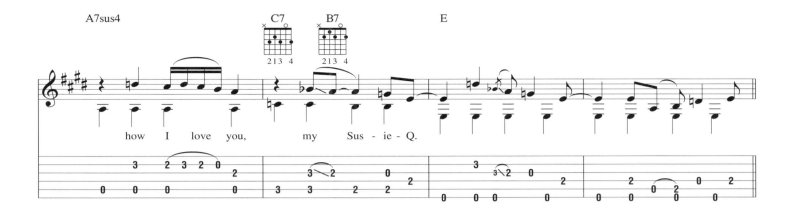

Here's the fingerpicking backup to "Train Kept A-Rollin'." It makes a good monotone bass exercise.

TRACK 21

TRAIN KEPT A-ROLLIN'—FINGERPICKING BACKUP

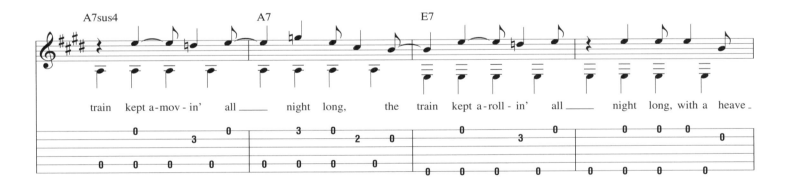

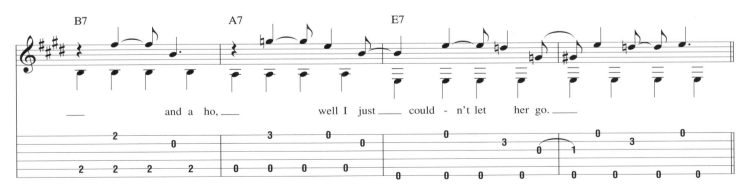

Moveable Chords

Merle Travis was one of the first fingerpickers to play moveable chords all over the fretboard, during solos and while accompanying singing. He was very popular in the late 1940s and 1950s, and rockabilly guitarists often imitate his style, albeit in a very bluesy vein and slightly simplified. Rockabilly guitarists often fingerpick moveable chords up the neck for accompaniment, especially favoring these chord shapes:

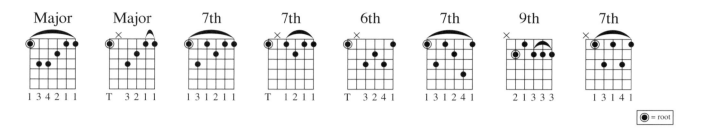

Some of these chord formations include the thumb, which wraps around the neck and holds down the sixth string. Countless blues, rockabilly, rock, and country guitarists play these "thumb" chords, but there are alternative ways to play them (shown above) if your thumb has trouble reaching the sixth string.

Some of these chord shapes have a sixth-string root, some have a fifth-string root, as marked in the above chord grids. To use these moveable chords all over the fretboard, it's necessary to know the notes on the fifth and sixth strings. Memorize the following diagram to take full advantage of these chord forms:

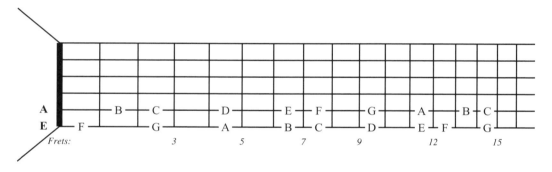

Scotty Moore fingerpicked some typical up-the-neck chords in "Milk Cow Blues." Elvis Presley's version of this 12-bar blues is based on a 1930s recording by Tennessean Sleepy John Estes. Robert Johnson also recorded a version of the tune, called "Milk Cow Calf Blues." Notice Moore's distinctive hammer-on figure, played on a sixth-string-root A7 chord. It's the main lick in his backup, played over and over.

TRACK 22

MILK COW BLUES—MOVEABLE CHORDS

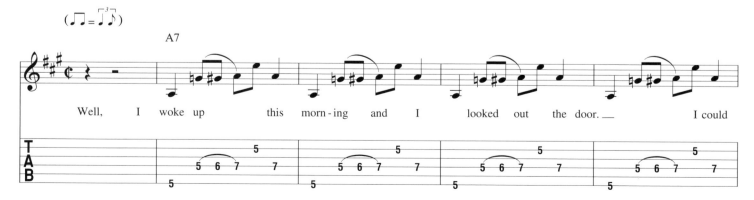

Words and Music by Kokomo Arnold
Copyright © 1934 UNIVERSAL MUSIC CORP.
Copyright Renewed
All Rights Reserved   Used by Permission

If Carl Perkins had fingerpicked backup while singing "Boppin' the Blues," it would have sounded something like this.

BOPPIN' THE BLUES—MOVEABLE CHORDS

CHOP CHORDS

Rockabilly guitarists often use *chop chords* for backup. These are abbreviated chords, usually played on the top four strings (the treble strings) that are clipped, or muted, for percussive effect; they punctuate the rhythm. The left hand does the muting by easing the pressure off the fretted strings right after picking the chord. For example, play an F formation at the fifth fret, which is an A chord. Right after strumming the chord, lift up the fretting fingers so that they are no longer fretting the strings but are still touching them. It should sound like this:

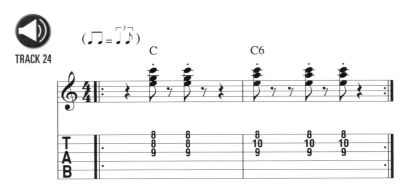

Danny Cedrone played a very repetitive chop chord rhythm pattern to "Rock Around the Clock." This 1954 hit by Bill Haley & His Comets is sometimes cited as the first rock 'n' roll record. That's debatable, but the song had a huge impact both in the U.S. and Britain, especially after its use in the 1955 movie, *The Blackboard Jungle*. It became a symbol of the new teenage music, just as "Staying Alive" spearheaded the disco craze, and it ultimately became the biggest-selling vinyl rock record of all time.

During one section of "Dance to the Bop," Johnny Meeks strummed moveable chords, and they were mostly chop chords.

DANCE TO THE BOP—CHOP CHORDS

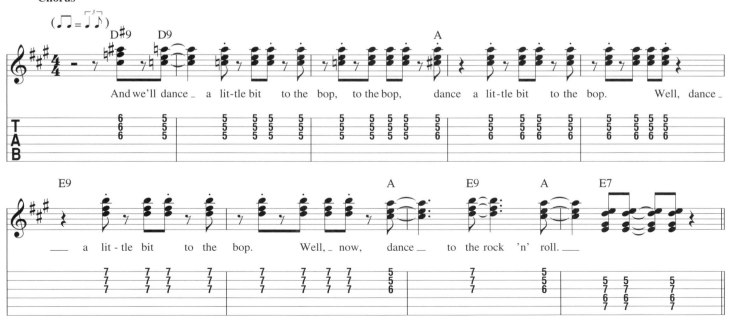

CHORD-BASED FILLS

During verses, the rockabilly rhythm guitarist strums a solid beat while the lead guitarist creates musical textures. You've already seen how this can be done with boogie bass lines, fingerpicking licks, and chop chords. Another way to add to the musical background is to play chord-based licks, or *fills*, during pauses in the vocal line.

To play chord-based fills, you follow a song's chord changes, usually playing abbreviated chords (two-, three-, or four-note chords) on the treble strings. You can also make up licks by slightly altering each chord shape. You might raise one note in the chord by hammering on, or you may slide up to the chord from one fret back. There's no end to the chord-based licks or variations that can be spun.

In "Race with the Devil," Cliff Gallup plays almost exactly the same intricate set of backup licks behind each of Gene Vincent's verses. Most of the licks are based on the F formation, which he played at the twelfth fret for an E chord and at the fifth and seventh frets for the A and B chords, respectively. He also played a D formation (the first-position D chord played anywhere on the neck) E lick at two points during each 12-measure verse. For the second solo, the band *modulated* (changed keys) to the key of F—an unusual move for a rockabilly band—and Gallup continued the same backup part, changing the open E licks to F licks at the first fret.

TRACK 26

RACE WITH THE DEVIL—CHORD-BASED FILLS

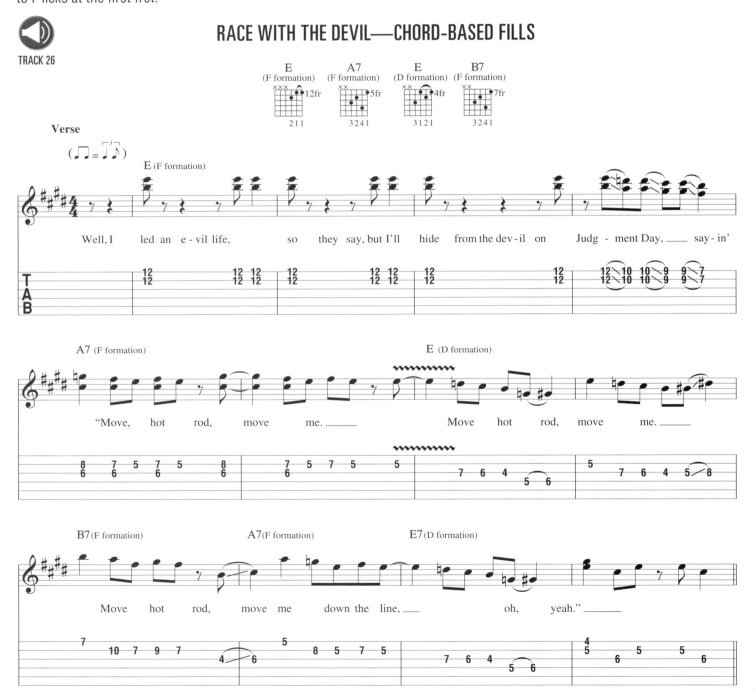

By Gene Vincent
© 1956 (Renewed 1984) BEECHWOOD MUSIC CORP.
All Rights Reserved   International Copyright Secured   Used by Permission

Between Brian Setzer's vocals in "Rock This Town," he occasionally plays chord-based fills. It's an especially useful technique for him in Stray Cats arrangements, as the band has no rhythm guitarist, and chord-based licks fill up space more than single-note solos.

ROCK THIS TOWN—CHORD-BASED FILLS

TRACK 27

SOLOING

Every guitar solo is based on something: a scale, a chord position, or a series of scales and chord positions. There's always a strategy involved, and sometimes several different strategies are employed in a 20-second solo. Here are the soloing strategies used most often by rockabilly lead guitarists.

FIRST-POSITION E MINOR PENTATONIC SCALE

Many early acoustic and electric blues guitarists played in the key of E most of the time; when E didn't suit their voice on a particular song, they used a capo. If A was a better singing key, they'd capo up five frets and play their favorite E licks and chords (when you play a first-position E chord capoed at the fifth fret, it sounds like A). Jimmy Reed, Lightnin' Hopkins (a big influence on fellow Texan Buddy Holly), Muddy Waters, and many other blues giants fit this description. So did Arthur Crudup, from whom Elvis got "That's All Right Mama."

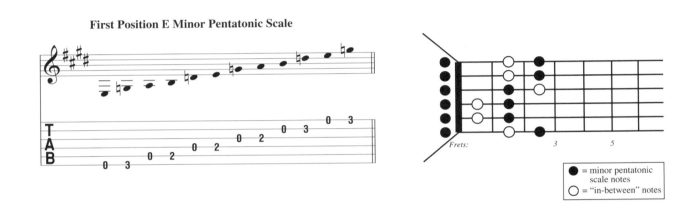

First Position E Minor Pentatonic Scale

● = minor pentatonic scale notes
○ = "in-between" notes

The reasons E is such an excellent blues key becomes apparent when you play a first-position E minor pentatonic scale:

- Every other note (not counting the "in-between notes") is an open string.

- The open sixth and fifth strings are handy bass notes for the E and A chords.

- The open third string is a blue note, a ♭3rd, and if you fret it at the first fret (as you do when playing an E major chord), it's a major 3rd. This is useful as the blues is neither major nor minor—it has elements of both—and you can state this tension just by playing the open third string and hammering onto the first fret:

The guitar riffs that hold "Susie-Q" and the Elvis tune "Little Sister" together are just two examples of classic rockabilly uses of the first-position E minor pentatonic scale. This scale is also the basis for many solos, such as Buddy Holly's instrumental break in "I'm Lookin' for Someone to Love" (below). Buddy played the same solo in an instrumental called "Holly Hop" that he used to open and close shows. The version that follows is slightly simplified, as Buddy fingerpicked parts of it (we'll get to that later!). Be sure to capo at the fifth fret for this one.

TRACK 28

I'M LOOKIN' FOR SOMEONE TO LOVE—FIRST POSITION

Capo V

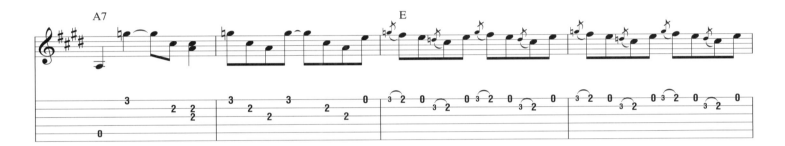

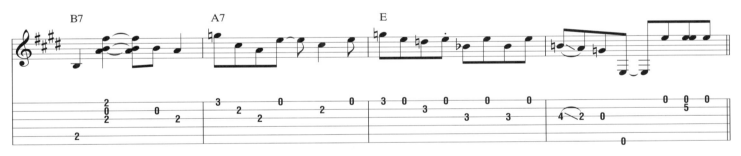

Words and Music by Buddy Holly and Norman Petty
© 1957 (Renewed) MPL MUSIC PUBLISHING, INC. and WREN MUSIC CO.
All Rights Reserved

The following solo to "Be-Bop-A-Lula" includes plenty of typical rockabilly licks, including string bending and triplets, and is based entirely on the first-position E minor pentatonic scale. While the 12-bar blues changes from one chord to the next, the soloist plays E minor pentatonic scale licks throughout. That's one great feature of soloing with this scale: you *don't* have to change positions or scales with the chord changes.

BE-BOP-A-LULA—FIRST POSITION

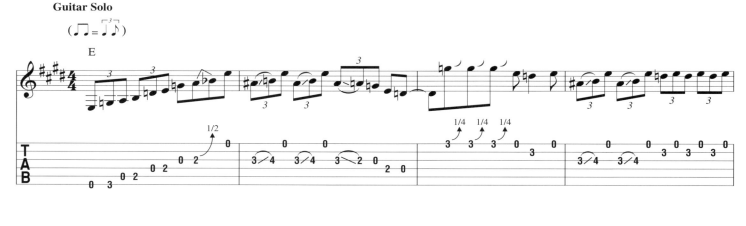

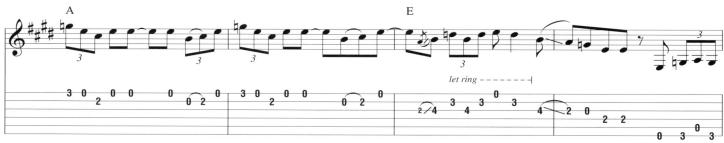

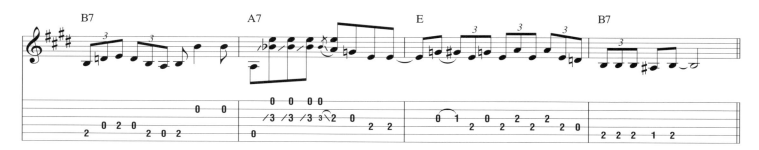

THE MOVEABLE BLUES BOX

Also known as the minor pentatonic scale, the scale position written below is the favorite soloing device of many blues, rock, and rockabilly lead guitarists. The expression "blues box" refers to the box-like shape the dots make when you map out the minor pentatonic scale on a fretboard. It evolved from the first-position E minor pentatonic scale when T-Bone Walker and a few other electric guitarists of the late 1930s found ways to play the classic key-of-E blues licks up the neck, in any key.

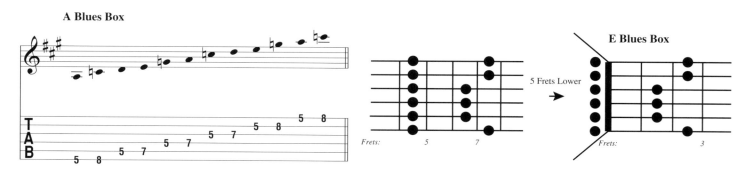

Since there are no open strings in this scale pattern, it can be played in any key. The first note of the scale (on the sixth string) is the root, so place the blues box in other keys by finding your root on the sixth string. For example, play in C by starting the blues box at the sixth string, eighth fret, which is the C note:

C Blues Box

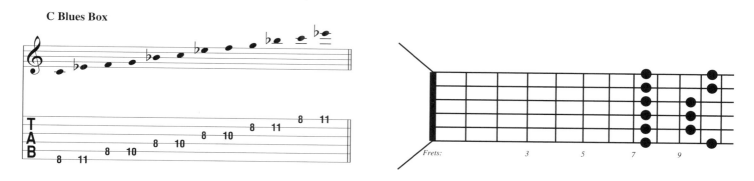

Here's how that first-position "Be-Bop-A-Lula" solo sounds when it's played in the key of A, using the moveable blues box. It's exactly the same as the first-position solo, but, since we're in fifth position, there are no open strings and it's in a different key.

TRACK 30

BE-BOP-A-LULA—MOVEABLE BLUES BOX

Guitar Solo

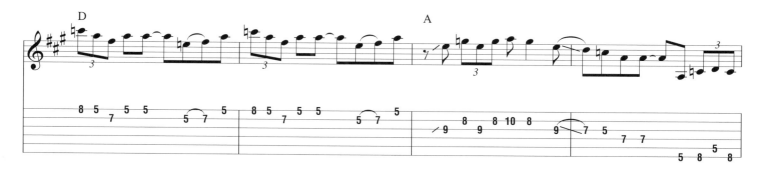

You can locate the appropriate blues box for a song by placing the F formation (the first-position F chord, shown below) in the right place. For example, the F formation at the third fret is a G chord, so finger this chord with your fretting hand to get "in position" for the G blues box:

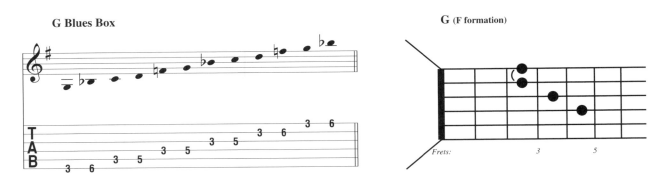

G Blues Box

G (F formation)

This F formation is a very important one in rockabilly, rock, blues, jazz, and country guitar. In fact, early blues players who developed the use of the moveable blues box were thinking more of the F shape than of the minor pentatonic scale because they included plenty of F-formation arpeggios and major scale notes along with the blue notes of the pentatonic scale.

You can play licks based on the F shape like this:

TRACK 31

Then add some nearby major scale notes:

TRACK 31
(0:13)

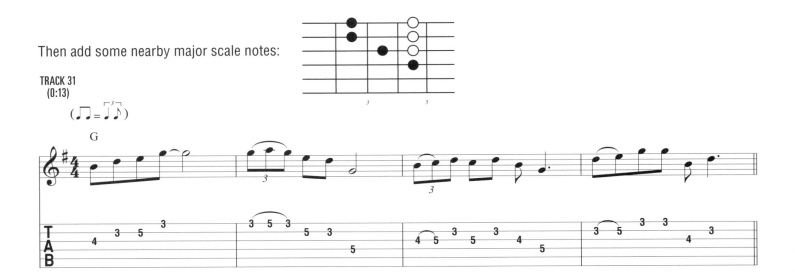

And finally, mix in some blue notes:

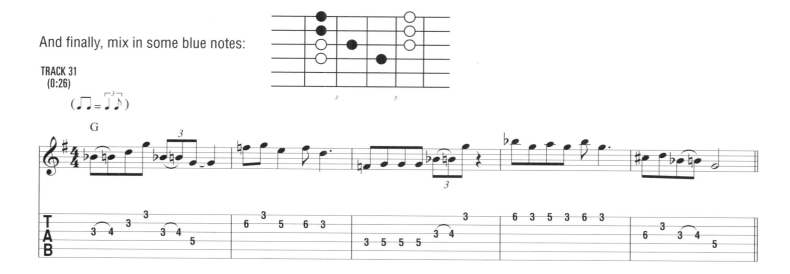

Here's Cliff Gallup's solo in Gene Vincent's hit, "Be-Bop-A-Lula." It's in the key of E, so the F-shaped E chord at the twelfth fret (or the blues box at the twelfth fret) is the basis for the entire solo. Gallup, considered by many to be the most advanced of the early rockabilly players, mixed major scale notes that are not included in the blues box with blue notes, giving his solos more of a jazz vibe than many rockabilly players.

BE-BOP-A-LULA—MOVEABLE BLUES BOX

Guitar Solo

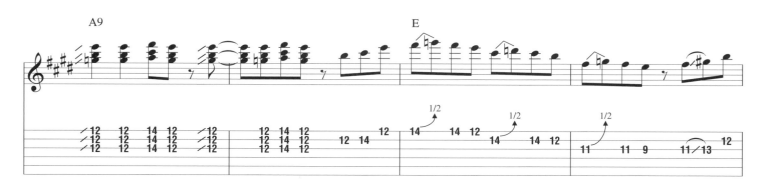

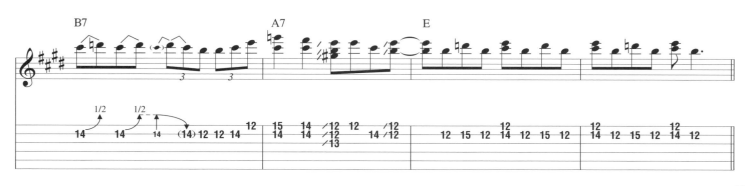

Gallup's first solo in "Race with the Devil" is also in E and is based on the F shape at the twelfth fret (or twelfth-fret blues box). The ascending lick at the end of the solo, which goes chromatically from the B chord to E, breaks out of the blues box. Gallup plays the F-shaped B chord at the seventh fret and slides up, one fret at a time, to arrive at the twelfth-fret E chord.

TRACK 33

RACE WITH THE DEVIL—MOVEABLE BLUES BOX

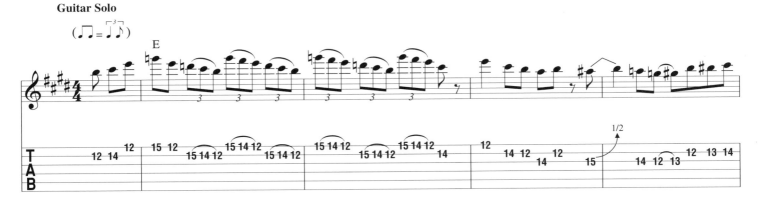

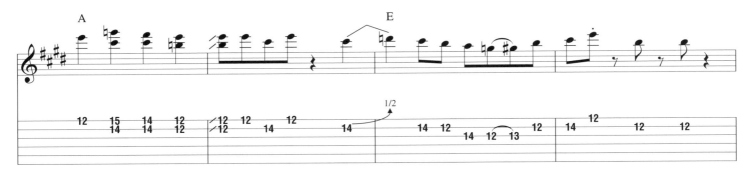

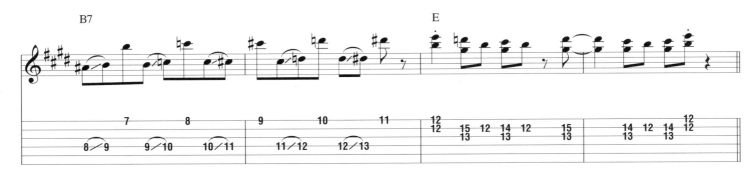

By Gene Vincent
© 1956 (Renewed 1984) BEECHWOOD MUSIC CORP.
All Rights Reserved   International Copyright Secured   Used by Permission

CHUCK BERRY-STYLE DOUBLE-NOTE LICKS

Chuck Berry has said that he based his guitar style, which influenced so many rockabilly guitarists, on the playing of T-Bone Walker. One of the key features of his sound is the use of "double-notes" (also called *doublestops*). He found pairs of notes within the moveable blues box:

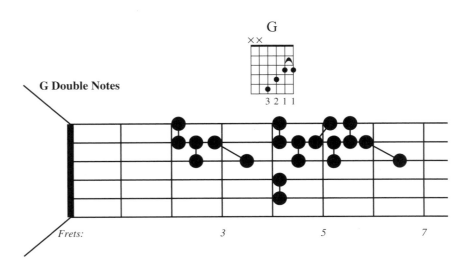

G Double Notes

Here are some typical Chuck Berry-style, double-note licks. To get your fretting hand "in position" to play them, play the moveable F formation G chord:

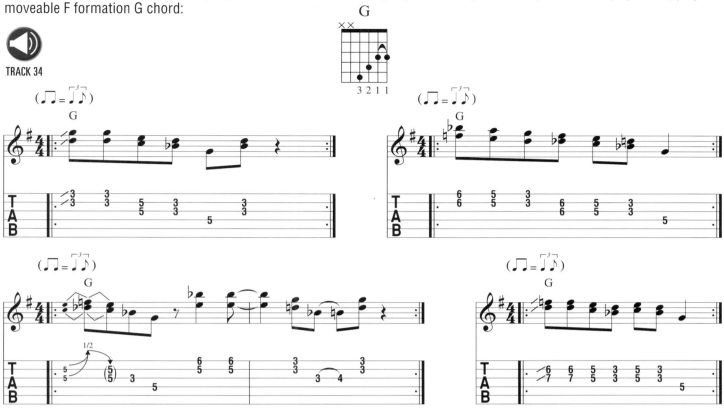

Sometimes Berry used his double-note licks to imitate his singing. For example, in "No Particular Place to Go," you can duplicate the vocal phrases with guitar fills.

NO PARTICULAR PLACE TO GO—DOUBLE-NOTE LICKS

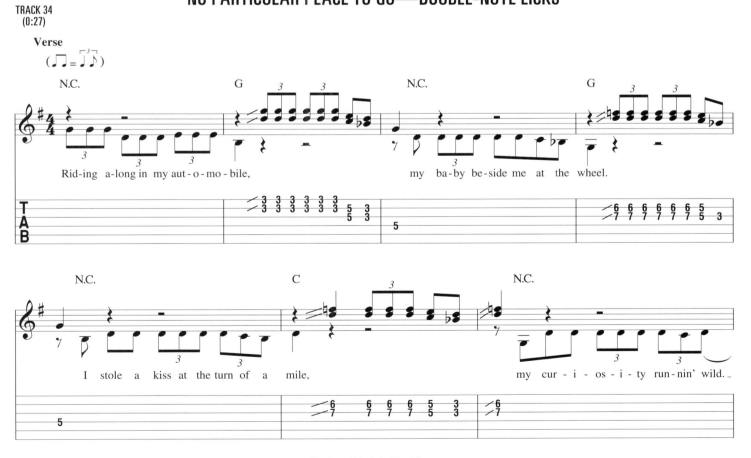

Words and Music by Chuck Berry
Copyright © 1964 (Renewed) by Arc Music Corp. (BMI)
Arc Music Corp. Administered by BMG Chrysalis for the world excluding Japan and Southeast Asia
All Rights Reserved   Used by Permission

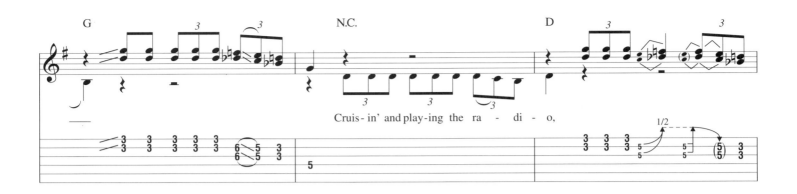

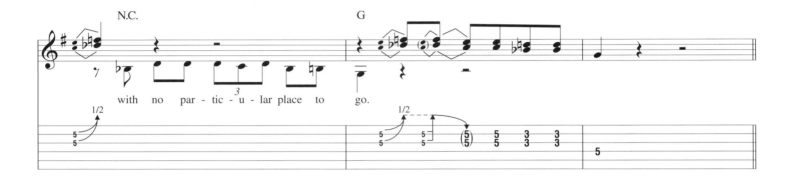

Chuck Berry's solos in "No Particular Place to Go" were very repetitive and entirely built on double- and, sometimes, triple-note licks. Here's his outro solo from the original recording of the tune. It begins with a full pick-up measure.

TRACK 35

NO PARTICULAR PLACE TO GO—DOUBLE-NOTE LICKS

Outro-Guitar Solo

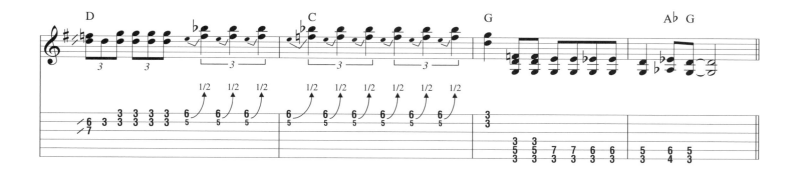

Rockabilly players often mix in double-note licks with their blues box-based solos. For example, here's Johnny Meeks's guitar solo in "Dance to the Bop." He took Cliff Gallup's place as lead guitarist for Gene Vincent.

DANCE TO THE BOP

TRACK 36

Guitar Solo

By Floyd Edge

As the last two solos illustrate, Berry and his guitar disciples usually stay in the I-chord position throughout a solo. If a tune is in C, the lead guitarist plays an F-formation C chord at the eighth fret and plays licks that are based on that position throughout the song's chord changes.

It's also possible to change soloing positions "with the changes." For example, look at (and listen to) the Blasters' lead guitar solo in "American Music." The soloist moves with the song's chord changes, playing F formations all the way.

TRACK 37

AMERICAN MUSIC—DOUBLE-NOTE LICKS

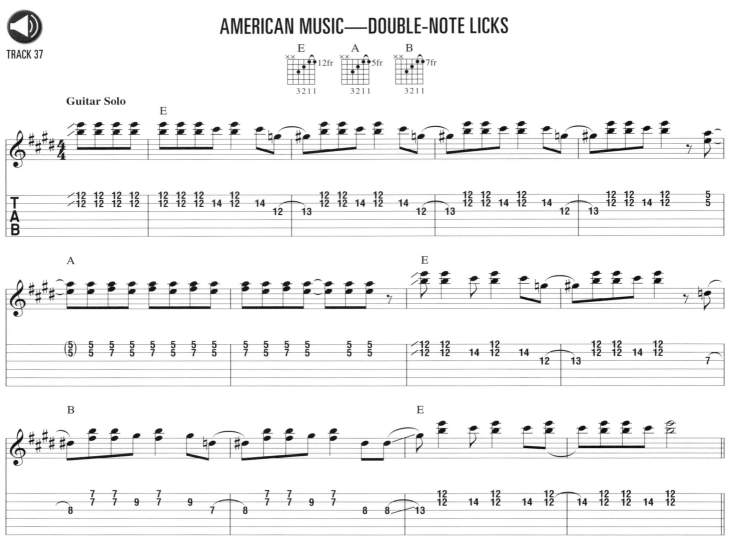

Written by Dave Alvin

CHORD-BASED SOLOING

Many rock and rockabilly solos are based on chords, rather than scales. A soloist can play a song's chord changes up and down the fretboard and construct licks out of each chord shape. They don't all have to be F formations, as they are in "American Music." In Buddy Holly's "Not Fade Away," Buddy based his solo on F and D formations up the neck. Buddy started out performing with just his guitar and a drummer, so he learned to solo with chords to fatten up the sound.

TRACK 38

NOT FADE AWAY—CHORD-BASED SOLOING

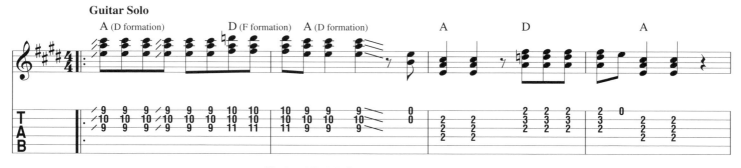

Words and Music by Charles Hardin and Norman Petty

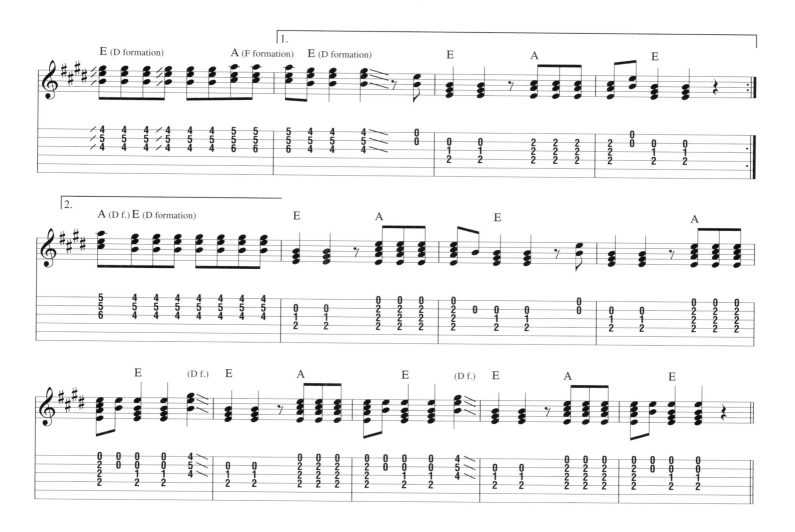

Carl Perkins' solo in "Honey Don't" is all chords, except for the boogie bass lines at the very end.

TRACK 39

HONEY DON'T—CHORD-BASED SOLOING

Perkins' solo in "Boppin' the Blues" is just as basic and totally chord-based.

TRACK 40

BOPPIN' THE BLUES—CHORD-BASED SOLOING

Words and Music by Carl Lee Perkins and Howard Griffin
© 1956 HI-LO MUSIC, INC.

FINGERPICKING SOLOS

Monotone Bass

In "Susie-Q," James Burton picked a steady, repetitive bass note on the open-E string for the song's signature riff (see "Fingerpicking Backup" section). Sometimes, rockabilly lead guitarists play melodic solos on the high strings while picking monotone bass notes. Here's how the solo to "Susie-Q" would sound if you fingerpicked the melody with a monotone bass.

SUSIE-Q—MELODIC SOLO WITH MONOTONE BASS

Guitar Solo

Words and Music by Dale Hawkins, Stan Lewis and Eleanor Broadwater
Copyright © 1957 (Renewed) by Arc Music Corp. (BMI)
Arc Music Corp. Administered by BMG Chrysalis for the world excluding Japan and Southeast Asia
All Rights Reserved   Used by Permission

James Burton did some monotone bass fingerpicking toward the end of his "Susie-Q" solo. The rest of the solo had a very acoustic country-blues flavor, as he played some Lightnin' Hopkins-style, key-of-E blues licks. The solo starts with a figure played on the top two strings at the seventh and eighth frets; this is sometimes called the "train whistle" lick since many acoustic blues pickers played it to imitate a train whistle.

SUSIE-Q—MELODIC SOLO WITH MONOTONE BASS

TRACK 41
(0:17)   **Guitar Solo**

Here's a melodic solo to "Train Kept A-Rollin'" that includes a monotone bass.

TRAIN KEPT A-ROLLIN'—MELODIC SOLO WITH MONOTONE BASS

Alternating Bass with First-Position Chords

Rockabilly lead guitarists fingerpick solos with alternating bass, à la Scotty Moore, more often than with monotone bass. Buddy Holly's solo in "I'm Lookin' for Someone to Love" is a good example. You played Buddy's first solo earlier, somewhat simplified (minus the bass). Here's his second solo, which has more alternating bass than the first. This transcription is complete and is a good study/exercise in this type of picking.

 I'M LOOKIN' FOR SOMEONE TO LOVE—ALTERNATING BASS WITH FIRST-POSITION CHORDS

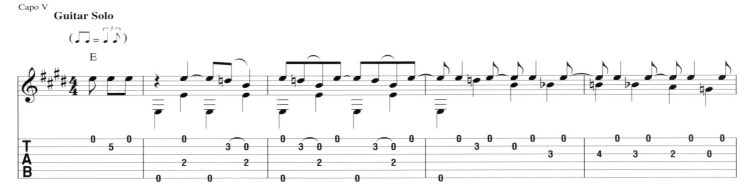

Alternating Bass with Moveable Chords

One of Merle Travis's main claims to fame was his use of moveable chords (often jazz chords) while fingerpicking with an alternating bass. He fingerpicked popular songs from the 1920s, '30s, and '40s, as well as country and folk songs, playing all over the fretboard—and his thumb never stopped thumping away on the bass strings! Scotty Moore, Carl Perkins, and other rockabilly pioneers incorporated this sound into rockabilly music, and it has always been a key sound in rockabilly lead guitar. Here are two classic examples from Elvis Presley's Sun Sessions: a Scotty Moore-style solo for "Good Rockin' Tonight" and Scotty's actual "Milk Cow Blues" solo.

TRACK 44

GOOD ROCKIN' TONIGHT—ALTERNATING BASS WITH MOVEABLE CHORDS

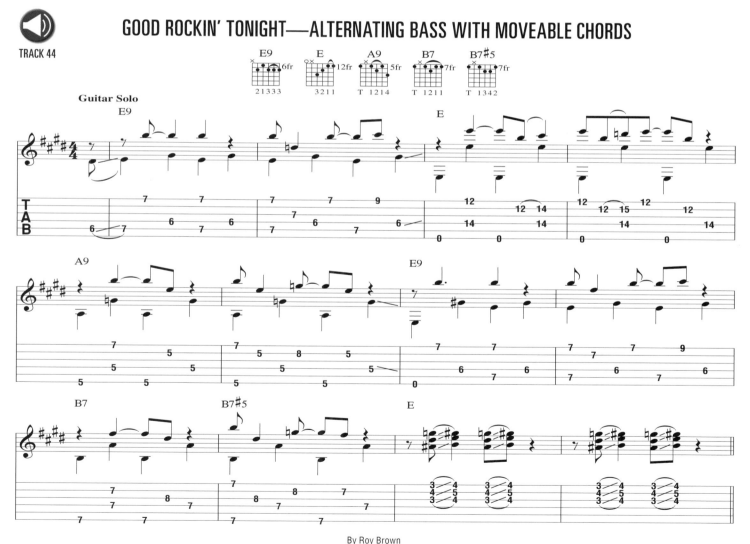

MILK COW BLUES—ALTERNATING BASS WITH MOVEABLE CHORDS

Cliff Gallup fingerpicked most of his second solo in Gene Vincent's hit, "Be-Bop-A-Lula."

TRACK 46

BE-BOP-A-LULA—ALTERNATING BASS WITH MOVEABLE CHORDS

SWING-STYLE SINGLE-NOTE SOLOING

In the 1950s, the guitarists who would come to be known as rockabilly pioneers were naturally listening to the famous guitarists of the day, including blues, country, R&B, and jazz players. Les Paul, Barney Kessel, and Tal Farlow were the prominent jazz guitarists, as were western swing pickers like Eldon Shamblin, Jimmy Wyble, and Junior Barnard, all of whom played at various times with Bob Wills. These virtuosos were adept at playing *single-note solos* in the electric jazz guitar tradition pioneered by Charlie Christian. Their influence is heard in the jazzy phrasing that sometimes flavored rockabilly solos.

Cliff Gallup's solos, in particular, show a swing influence. His timing is often surprising, and he flavors major scale licks with blue notes in a style reminiscent of jazz guitarists. His second solo in "Race with the Devil" is a good example of his jazzy style. (The first solo [see pg. 40] also has jazzy phrasing.) Nearly all the licks are generated from the F chord within the first three frets, and most of the notes surrounding that position are played, as well as the notes of the F chord itself.

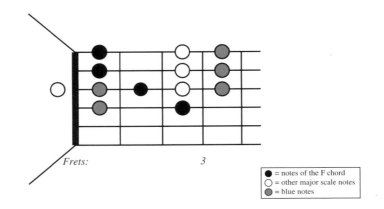

Frets: 3

● = notes of the F chord
○ = other major scale notes
● = blue notes

RACE WITH THE DEVIL—SWING-STYLE SOLOING

TRACK 47

Guitar Solo

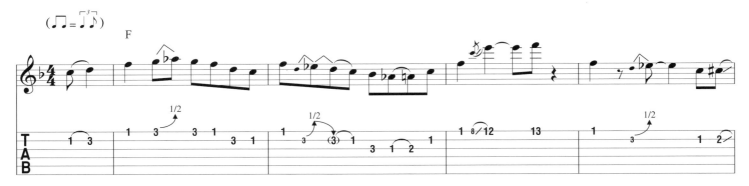

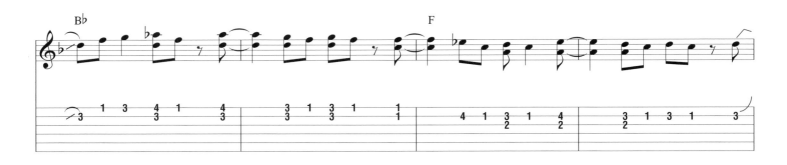

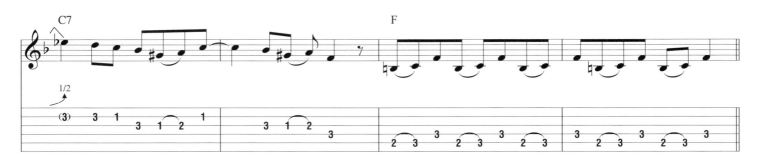

By Gene Vincent
© 1956 (Renewed 1984) BEECHWOOD MUSIC CORP.
All Rights Reserved   International Copyright Secured   Used by Permission

Danny Cedrone, whose break in "Rock Around the Clock" is one of the most famous solos in rock guitar history, was not a "rockabilly cat." Born in New York, he was a 34-year-old session player in 1954 when he recorded the tune with Bill Haley and His Comets. His solo duplicated one he recorded a few years earlier with Haley, in the song "Rock the Joint."

The rapid-fire, repetitive riffs sound jazzier than most early rock, and that speedy, chromatic lick at the end of the solo is unusual and ear-catching. Like the "Race with the Devil" solo, most of this break is based on the F formation (in this case, played at the fifth fret, as the song is in the key of A).

ROCK AROUND THE CLOCK—SWING-STYLE SOLOING

TRACK 48

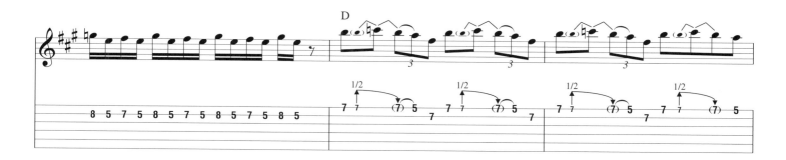

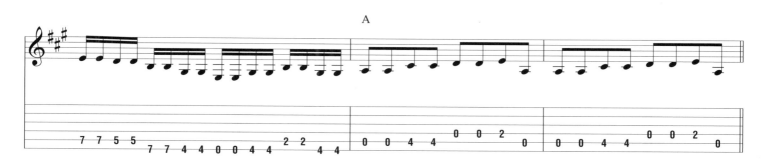

Words and Music by Max C. Freedman and Jimmy DeKnight
Copyright © 1953 Myers Music Inc. and Capano Music
Copyright Renewed 1981
All Rights on behalf of Myers Music Inc. Administered by Sony/ATV Music Publishing LLC, 8 Music Square West, Nashville, TN 37203
International Copyright Secured   All Rights Reserved

Brian Setzer knows all the classic rockabilly licks and often quotes them in his solos, but his break in "Rock This Town" is very original, jazzy, and displays a variety of styles. It's based mostly around the F formation at the tenth fret (he's in the key of D), but also makes use of the D *major pentatonic scale* played often by rockers, as well as jazz and country guitarists.

TRACK 49

ROCK THIS TOWN—SWING-STYLE SOLOING

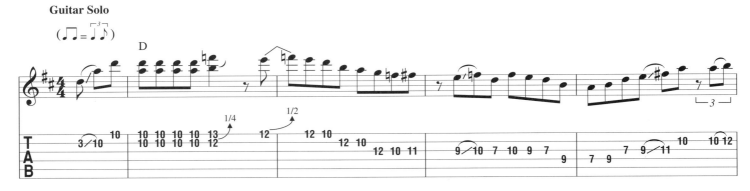

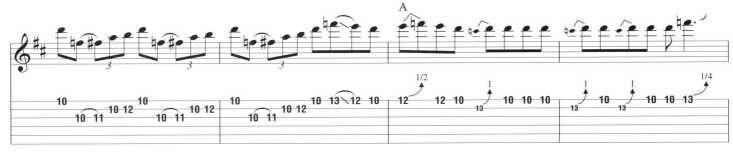

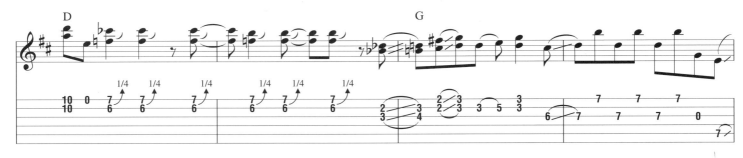

OCTAVE SOLOING

Octave soloing is associated with jazz more than rockabilly. Django Reinhardt sometimes sprinkled his solos with octaves, and Wes Montgomery was famous for playing extended solos with octaves. Cliff Gallup's climbing octaves at the end of the first solo in "Race with the Devil" is the exception that proves the rule. Paul Burlison provided another exception in "Train Kept A-Rollin'" when he played rarely-heard double octaves throughout the tune. They were the same first- and sixth-string octaves Montgomery later popularized in his crossover hit, "Bumpin' on Sunset." Here are two possible fingerings for an octave G note:

Here's Burlison's novelty double-octave solo.

TRACK 50

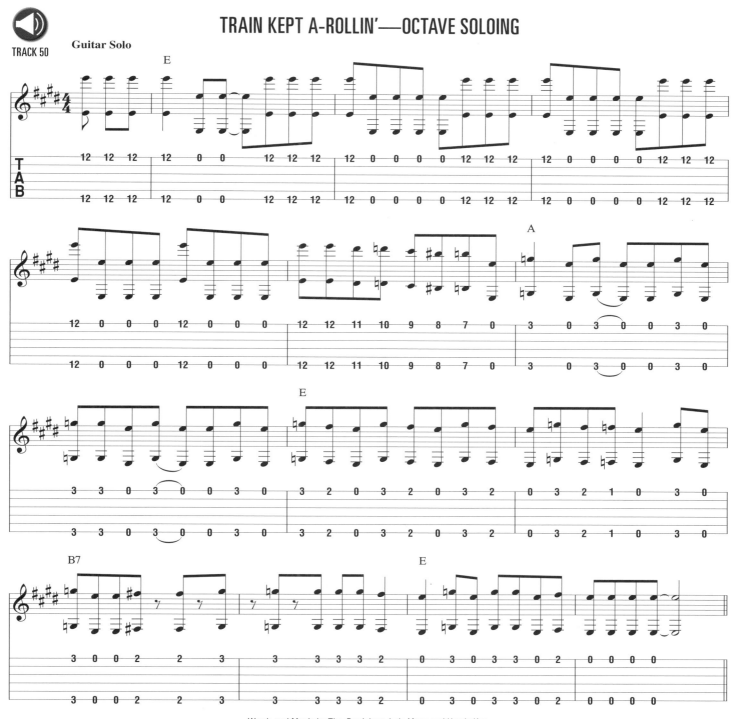

TRAIN KEPT A-ROLLIN'—OCTAVE SOLOING

Guitar Solo

PSYCHOBILLY

A blend of rockabilly, punk, and metal, psychobilly is fast, high-energy, musically uncomplicated, and driven by loud, distorted guitars. The beginning of Reverend Horton Heat's "Psychobilly Freakout" is a good example. It's in E, a favorite rockabilly key, and features blues licks galore—but it's a long way from Carl Perkins to here!

PSYCHOBILLY FREAKOUT

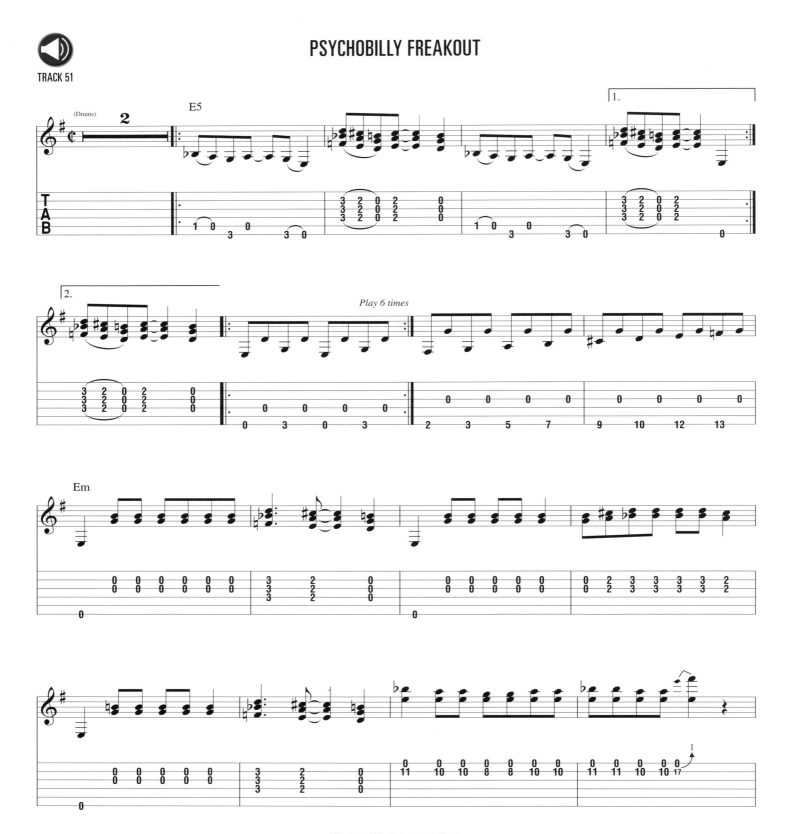

TRACK 51

Words and Music by James Heath
Copyright © 1990 Horton House Publishing
All Rights Reserved   Used by Permission

ENDINGS & CLOSING CHORDS: 6THS, 7THS, AND 6/9 CHORDS

Ending a blues with a 7th or 9th chord is standard procedure. In the blues, 7ths and 9ths are often played instead of major chords, so it's not surprising that some 1950s rockabilly guitarists ended tunes with 7ths or 9ths. Perhaps because they were listening to jazz guitarist Les Paul or Merle Travis (who often played jazz chords), the rockabilly pioneers often ended songs with a 6th chord or a jazzier 6/9 chord.

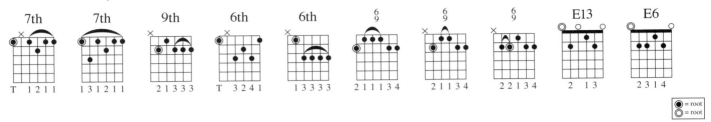

Here are several endings to classic rockabilly tunes. Many feature imaginative licks that lead up to the final chord.

TRACK 52

BOPPIN' THE BLUES—ENDING

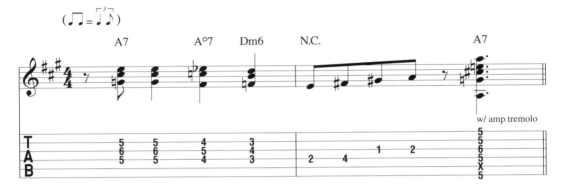

TRACK 53

HONEY DON'T—ENDING

TRACK 54

DANCE TO THE BOP—ENDING

ROCK AROUND THE CLOCK—ENDING

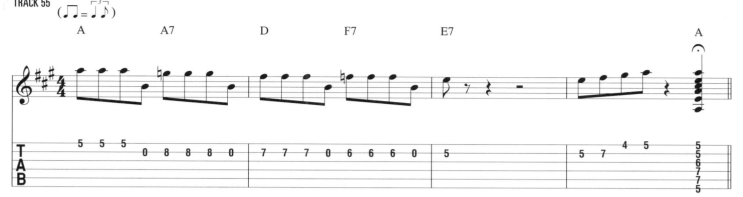

TRACK 56

BE-BOP-A-LULA—ENDING

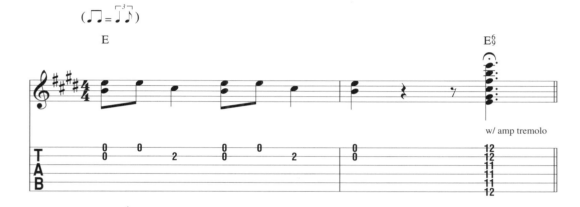

TRACK 57

ROCK THIS TOWN—ENDING

TRACK 58

RACE WITH THE DEVIL—ENDING

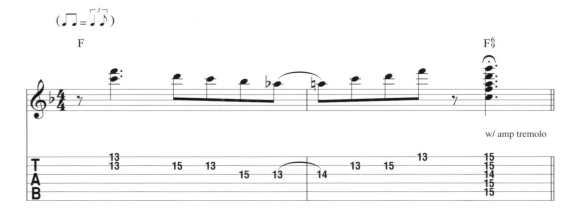

59

WHERE TO GO FROM HERE

After you've learned the tunes and exercises in this book, there are several things you can do to progress further as a rocka-billy player:

- **Listen to more rockabilly music.** This includes both the 1950s recordings and contemporary rockabilly bands, or bands that are influenced by rockabilly. Check the radio programming in your area for rockabilly programs.

- **Patronize the local clubs, bars, and concert halls that feature live rockabilly music.**

- **Find another guitarist, singer, upright bassist, and drummer who like this music and start jamming!** Playing music with other people is a lot more fun than practicing with recordings. It also illuminates your strengths and weaknesses, which helps you grow as a player.

- **Try out the techniques you've learned in this book on other songs.** Play more vintage rockabilly material; give rock, country, blues, or bluegrass songs a rockabilly treatment. Write your own rockabilly classics!

Go Cats!

Fred Sokolow

P.S.: Check out my website, *sokolowmusic.com*, for more Hal Leonard books that are rockabilly-related, such as:

Buddy Holly Recorded Versions
Chuck Berry Guitar Recorded Versions
Elvis Presley Recorded Versions
Classic Rock Guitar Instrumentals Guitar Recorded Versions

ABOUT THE AUTHOR

FRED SOKOLOW is a versatile "musician's musician." Besides fronting his own jazz, bluegrass, and rock bands, Fred has toured with Bobbie Gentry, Jim Stafford, Tom Paxton, Ian Whitcomb, Jody Stecher, and the Limeliters, playing guitar, banjo, mandolin, and Dobro. His music has been heard on many TV shows (*Survivor*, *Dr. Quinn*), commercials, and movies (listen for his Dixieland-style banjo in *The Cat's Meow*).

Sokolow has written over a hundred stringed-instrument books and videos for seven major publishers. This library of instructional material, which teaches jazz, rock, bluegrass, country, and blues guitar, banjo, Dobro, and mandolin, is sold on six continents. He also teaches musical seminars on the West Coast. Two jazz CDs, two rock guitar, and two banjo recordings, which showcase Sokolow's technique, all received excellent reviews in the U.S. and Europe.

If you think Sokolow still isn't versatile enough, know that he emceed for Carol Doda at San Francisco's legendary Condor Club, accompanied a Russian balalaika virtuoso at the swank Bonaventure Hotel in L.A., won the *Gong Show*, played lap steel and banjo on the *Tonight Show*, picked Dobro with Chubby Checker, and played mandolin with Rick James.

Direct questions you may have about this book or other Fred Sokolow books to *sokolowmusic.com*.

GUITAR NOTATION LEGEND

Guitar music can be notated three different ways: on a *musical staff*, in *tablature*, and in *rhythm slashes*.

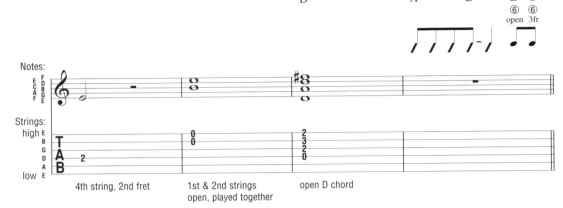

RHYTHM SLASHES are written above the staff. Strum chords in the rhythm indicated. Use the chord diagrams found at the top of the first page of the transcription for the appropriate chord voicings. Round noteheads indicate single notes.

THE MUSICAL STAFF shows pitches and rhythms and is divided by bar lines into measures. Pitches are named after the first seven letters of the alphabet.

TABLATURE graphically represents the guitar fingerboard. Each horizontal line represents a string, and each number represents a fret.

4th string, 2nd fret

1st & 2nd strings open, played together

open D chord

Definitions for Special Guitar Notation

HALF-STEP BEND: Strike the note and bend up 1/2 step.

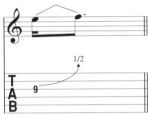

WHOLE-STEP BEND: Strike the note and bend up one step.

GRACE NOTE BEND: Strike the note and immediately bend up as indicated.

SLIGHT (MICROTONE) BEND: Strike the note and bend up 1/4 step.

BEND AND RELEASE: Strike the note and bend up as indicated, then release back to the original note. Only the first note is struck.

PRE-BEND: Bend the note as indicated, then strike it.

PRE-BEND AND RELEASE: Bend the note as indicated. Strike it and release the bend back to the original note.

UNISON BEND: Strike the two notes simultaneously and bend the lower note up to the pitch of the higher.

VIBRATO: The string is vibrated by rapidly bending and releasing the note with the fretting hand.

WIDE VIBRATO: The pitch is varied to a greater degree by vibrating with the fretting hand.

HAMMER-ON: Strike the first (lower) note with one finger, then sound the higher note (on the same string) with another finger by fretting it without picking.

PULL-OFF: Place both fingers on the notes to be sounded. Strike the first note and without picking, pull the finger off to sound the second (lower) note.

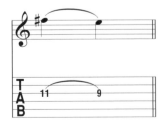

LEGATO SLIDE: Strike the first note and then slide the same fret-hand finger up or down to the second note. The second note is not struck.

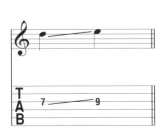

SHIFT SLIDE: Same as legato slide, except the second note is struck.

TRILL: Very rapidly alternate between the notes indicated by continuously hammering on and pulling off.

TAPPING: Hammer ("tap") the fret indicated with the pick-hand index or middle finger and pull off to the note fretted by the fret hand.

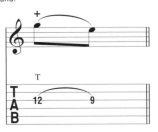

NATURAL HARMONIC: Strike the note while the fret-hand lightly touches the string directly over the fret indicated.

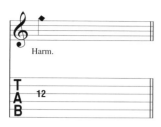

PINCH HARMONIC: The note is fretted normally and a harmonic is produced by adding the edge of the thumb or the tip of the index finger of the pick hand to the normal pick attack.

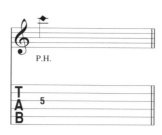

HARP HARMONIC: The note is fretted normally and a harmonic is produced by gently resting the pick hand's index finger directly above the indicated fret (in parentheses) while the pick hand's thumb or pick assists by plucking the appropriate string.

PICK SCRAPE: The edge of the pick is rubbed down (or up) the string, producing a scratchy sound.

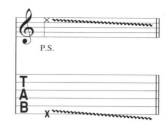

MUFFLED STRINGS: A percussive sound is produced by laying the fret hand across the string(s) without depressing, and striking them with the pick hand.

PALM MUTING: The note is partially muted by the pick hand lightly touching the string(s) just before the bridge.

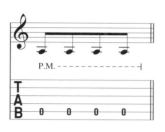

RAKE: Drag the pick across the strings indicated with a single motion.

TREMOLO PICKING: The note is picked as rapidly and continuously as possible.

ARPEGGIATE: Play the notes of the chord indicated by quickly rolling them from bottom to top.

VIBRATO BAR DIVE AND RETURN: The pitch of the note or chord is dropped a specified number of steps (in rhythm), then returned to the original pitch.

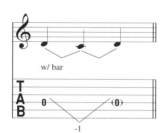

VIBRATO BAR SCOOP: Depress the bar just before striking the note, then quickly release the bar.

VIBRATO BAR DIP: Strike the note and then immediately drop a specified number of steps, then release back to the original pitch.

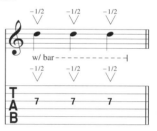

Definitions for Special Guitar Notation

(accent)	• Accentuate note (play it louder).	
(accent)	• Accentuate note with great intensity.	
(staccato)	• Play the note short.	
	• Downstroke	
	• Upstroke	

D.S. al Coda • Go back to the sign (%), then play until the measure marked "**To Coda**," then skip to the section labelled "**Coda**."

D.C. al Fine • Go back to the beginning of the song and play until the measure marked "*Fine*" (end).

Rhy. Fig. • Label used to recall a recurring accompaniment pattern (usually chordal).

Riff • Label used to recall composed, melodic lines (usually single notes) which recur.

Fill • Label used to identify a brief melodic figure which is to be inserted into the arrangement.

Rhy. Fill • A chordal version of a Fill.

tacet • Instrument is silent (drops out).

• Repeat measures between signs.

• When a repeated section has different endings, play the first ending only the first time and the second ending only the second time.

NOTE: Tablature numbers in parentheses mean:
   1. The note is being sustained over a system (note in standard notation is tied), or
   2. The note is sustained, but a new articulation (such as a hammer-on, pull-off, slide or vibrato) begins, or
   3. The note is a barely audible "ghost" note (note in standard notation is also in parentheses).

HAL LEONARD GUITAR METHOD

by Will Schmid and Greg Koch

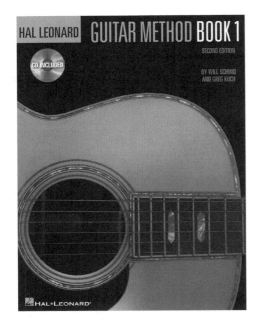

HAL LEONARD GUITAR METHOD BOOK 1
SECOND EDITION
CD INCLUDED
BY WILL SCHMID AND GREG KOCH

THE HAL LEONARD GUITAR METHOD is designed for anyone just learning to play acoustic or electric guitar. It is based on years of teaching guitar students of all ages, and it also reflects some of the best guitar teaching ideas from around the world. This comprehensive method includes: A learning sequence carefully paced with clear instructions; popular songs which increase the incentive to learn to play; versatility – can be used as self-instruction or with a teacher; audio accompaniments so that students have fun and sound great while practicing.

BOOK 1
00699010	Book	$7.99
00699027	Book with audio on CD & Online	$10.99
00137760	Deluxe Edition (with Online Audio & Video)	$14.99
00155480	Deluxe Beginner Pack (Book/DVD/CD/Online Audio & Video/Poster)	$19.99

BOOK 2
00699020	Book	$7.99
00697313	Book/CD Pack	$10.99

BOOK 3
00699030	Book	$7.99
00697316	Book/CD Pack	$9.95

COMPOSITE
Books 1, 2, and 3 bound together in an easy-to-use spiral binding.
00699040	Books Only	$14.99
00697342	Book/3-CD Pack	$24.99

DVD
FOR THE BEGINNING ELECTRIC OR ACOUSTIC GUITARIST
00697318	DVD	$19.95
00697341	Book/CD Pack and DVD	$24.99

GUITAR FOR KIDS
A BEGINNER'S GUIDE WITH STEP-BY-STEP INSTRUCTION FOR ACOUSTIC AND ELECTRIC GUITAR
by Bob Morris and Jeff Schroedl
00865003	Book 1 – Book/CD Pack	$12.99
00697402	Songbook Book/CD Pack	$9.99
00128437	Book 2 – Book/Online Audio	$12.99

SONGBOOKS

EASY POP MELODIES
00697281	Book	$6.99
00697268	Book/CD Pack	$14.99

MORE EASY POP MELODIES
00697280	Book	$6.99
00697269	Book/CD Pack	$14.99

EVEN MORE EASY POP MELODIES
00699154	Book	$6.99
00697270	Book/Online Audio	$14.99

EASY POP RHYTHMS
00697336	Book	$6.95
00697309	Book/CD Pack	$14.99

MORE EASY POP RHYTHMS
00697338	Book	$6.95
00697322	Book/CD Pack	$14.95

EVEN MORE EASY POP RHYTHMS
00697340	Book	$6.95
00697323	Book/CD Pack	$14.95

EASY SOLO GUITAR PIECES
00110407	Book	$9.99

EASY POP CHRISTMAS MELODIES
00697417	Book	$6.99
00697416	Book/CD Pack	$14.99

LEAD LICKS
00697345	Book/CD Pack	$9.99

RHYTHM RIFFS
00697346	Book/CD Pack	$9.95

STYLISTIC METHODS

ACOUSTIC GUITAR
00697347	Book/CD Pack	$16.95
00697384	Acoustic Guitar Songs	$14.95

BLUEGRASS GUITAR
00697405	Book/CD Pack	$16.99

BLUES GUITAR
00697326	Book/CD Pack	$16.99
00697385	Blues Guitar Songs (with Online Audio)	$14.95

BRAZILIAN GUITAR
00697415	Book/CD Pack	$14.99

CHRISTIAN GUITAR
00695947	Book/CD Pack	$12.99
00697408	Christian Guitar Songs	$14.99

CLASSICAL GUITAR
00697376	Book/CD Pack	$14.99
00697388	Classical Guitar Pieces	$9.99

COUNTRY GUITAR
00697337	Book/CD Pack	$22.99
00697400	Country Guitar Songs	$14.99

FINGERSTYLE GUITAR
00697378	Book/CD Pack	$19.99
00697432	Fingerstyle Guitar Songs (with Online Audio)	$14.99

FLAMENCO GUITAR
00697363	Book/CD Pack	$14.99

FOLK GUITAR
00697414	Book/CD Pack	$14.99

JAZZ GUITAR
00695359	Book/CD Pack	$19.99
00697386	Jazz Guitar Songs	$14.95

JAZZ-ROCK FUSION
00697387	Book/CD Pack	$19.99

ROCK GUITAR
00697319	Book/CD Pack	$16.95
00697383	Rock Guitar Songs	$14.95

ROCKABILLY GUITAR
00697407	Book/CD Pack	$16.95

R&B GUITAR
00697356	Book/CD Pack	$14.95
00697433	R&B Guitar Songs	$14.95

REFERENCE

ARPEGGIO FINDER
00697352	6" x 9" Edition	$5.99
00697351	9" x 12" Edition	$6.99

INCREDIBLE CHORD FINDER
00697200	6" x 9" Edition	$5.99
00697208	9" x 12" Edition	$6.99

INCREDIBLE SCALE FINDER
00695568	6" x 9" Edition	$5.99
00695490	9" x 12" Edition	$6.99

GUITAR CHORD, SCALE & ARPEGGIO FINDER
00697410		$19.99

GUITAR SETUP & MAINTENANCE
00697427	6" x 9" Edition	$14.99
00697421	9" x 12" Edition	$12.99

GUITAR TECHNIQUES
00697389	Book/CD Pack	$12.95

GUITAR PRACTICE PLANNER
00697401		$5.99

MUSIC THEORY FOR GUITARISTS
00695790	Book/Online Audio	$19.99

HAL•LEONARD CORPORATION
7777 W. BLUEMOUND RD. P.O. BOX 13819 MILWAUKEE, WI 53213
www.halleonard.com

Prices, contents and availability subject to change without notice.